National Gallery of Art

Washington, DC

Distributed by Rizzoli Electa, New York

Selected Works

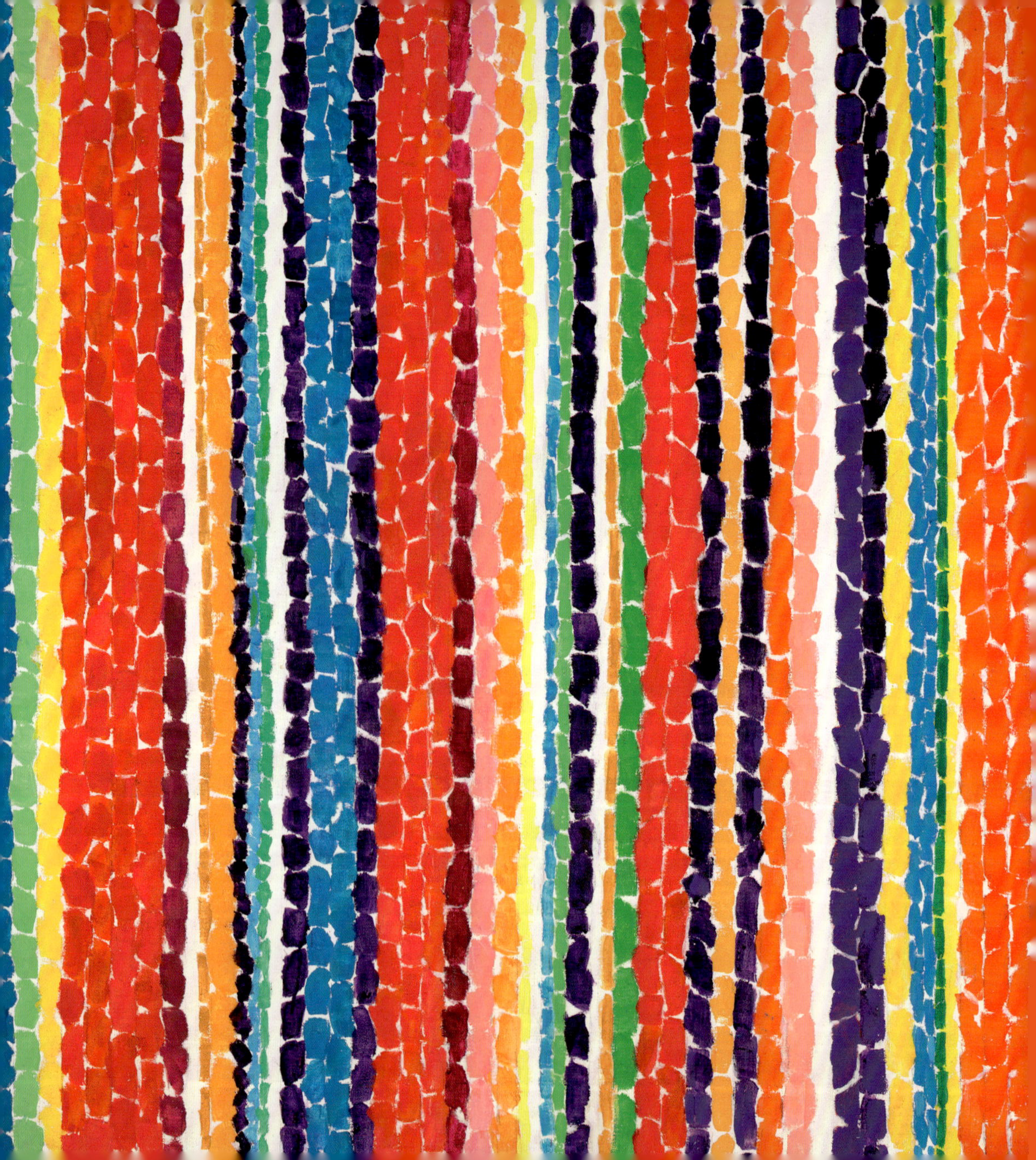

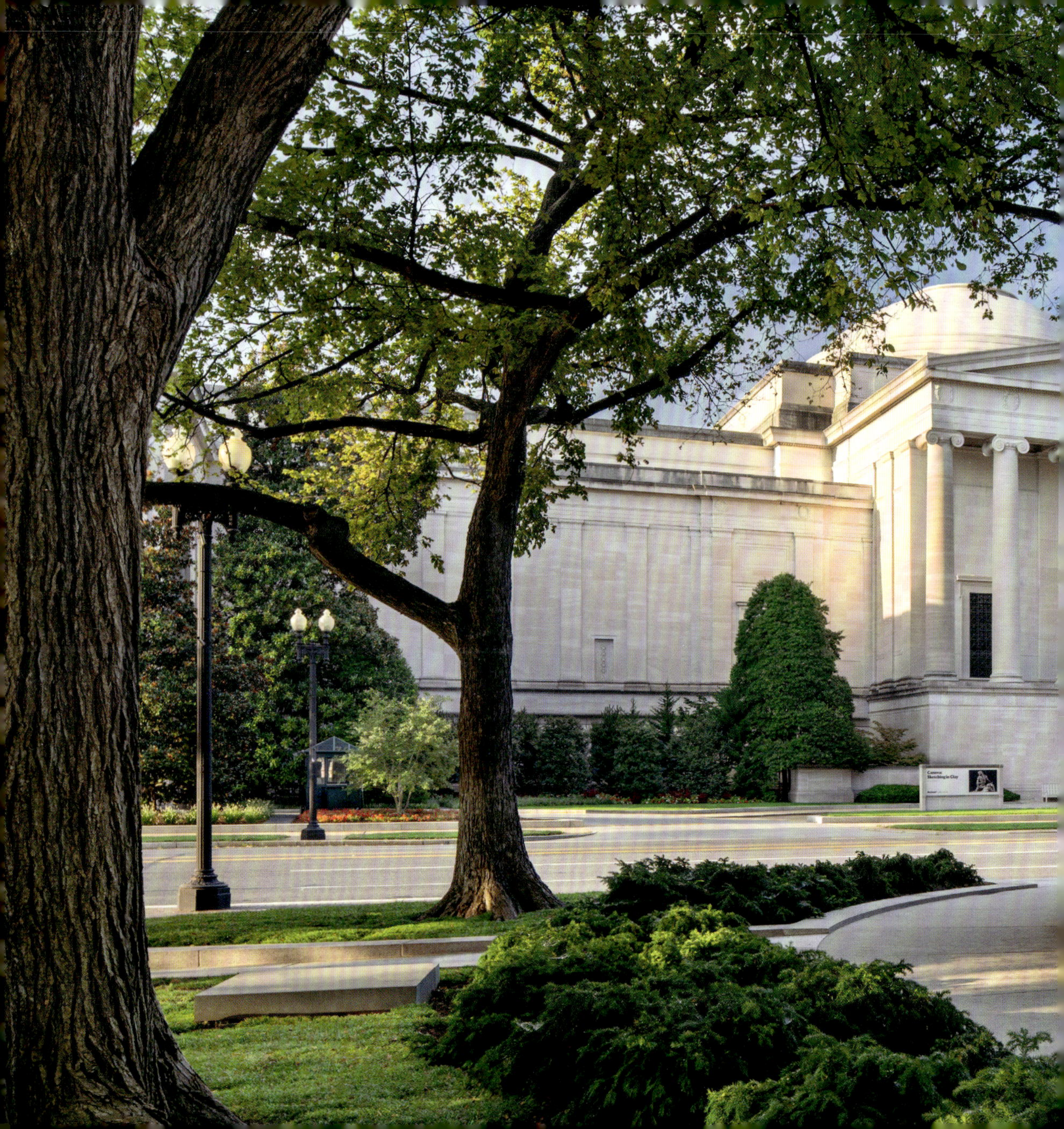

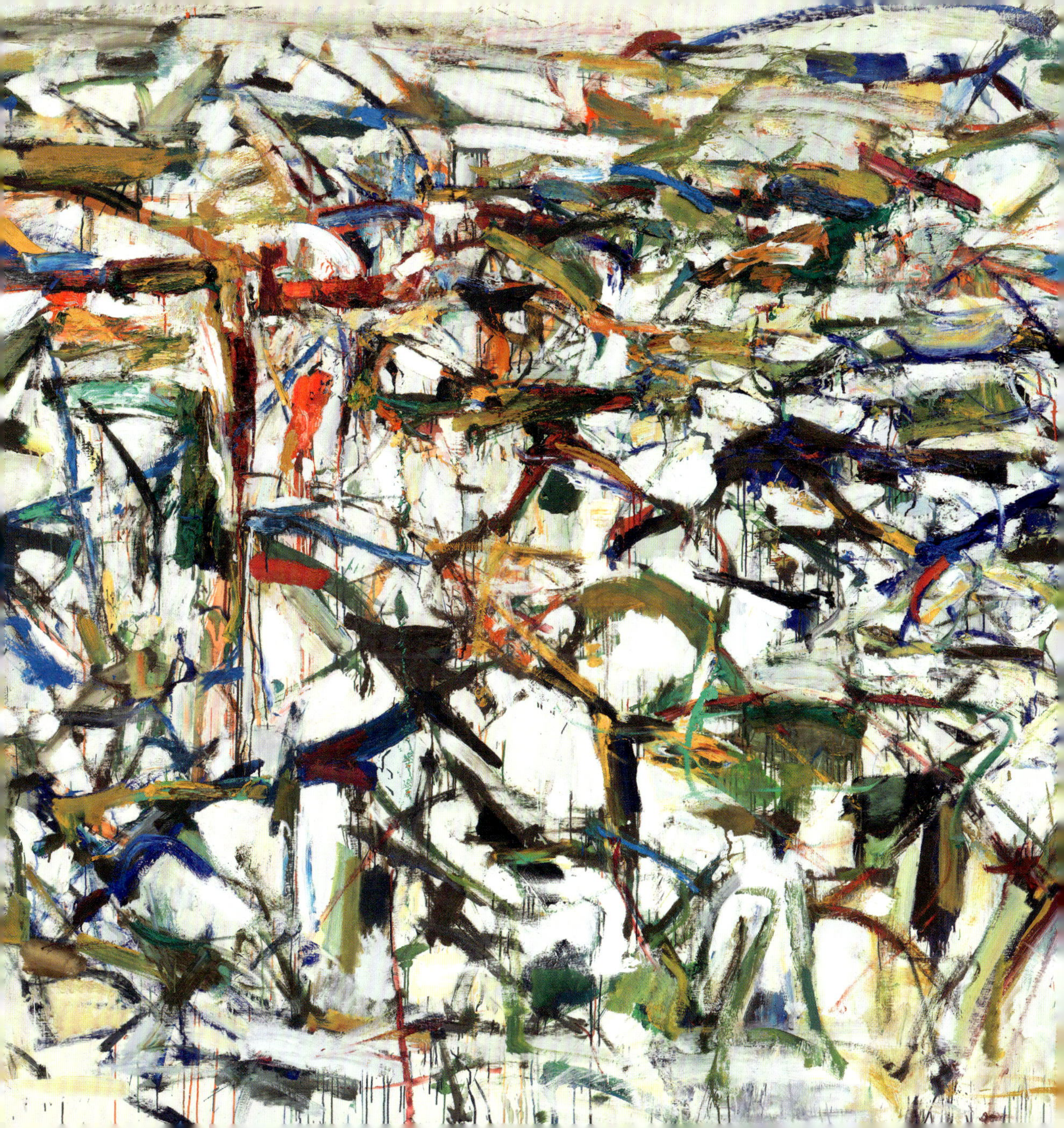

Director's Welcome

Welcome to the National Gallery of Art, where art is yours to discover and explore.

Our collection includes more than 150,000 paintings, sculptures, works of decorative art, photographs, prints, and drawings—and we're still growing. The works in the National Gallery span over a thousand years of the history of European and American art. And as you'll see in this book, they showcase numerous triumphs of human creativity.

From the thousands of objects in the National Gallery's collection, we've selected more than 50 remarkable works of art. Many represent self-exploration and identity, emotion and spirituality. Others are quiet memorials to the everyday that connect us in our common understanding of the world.

I believe art has the power to make a difference in our lives. That concept is central to the National Gallery's mission to serve the nation by welcoming all people to explore and experience art, creativity, and our shared humanity.

Come and see what art can do for you.

Kaywin Feldman
Director, National Gallery of Art

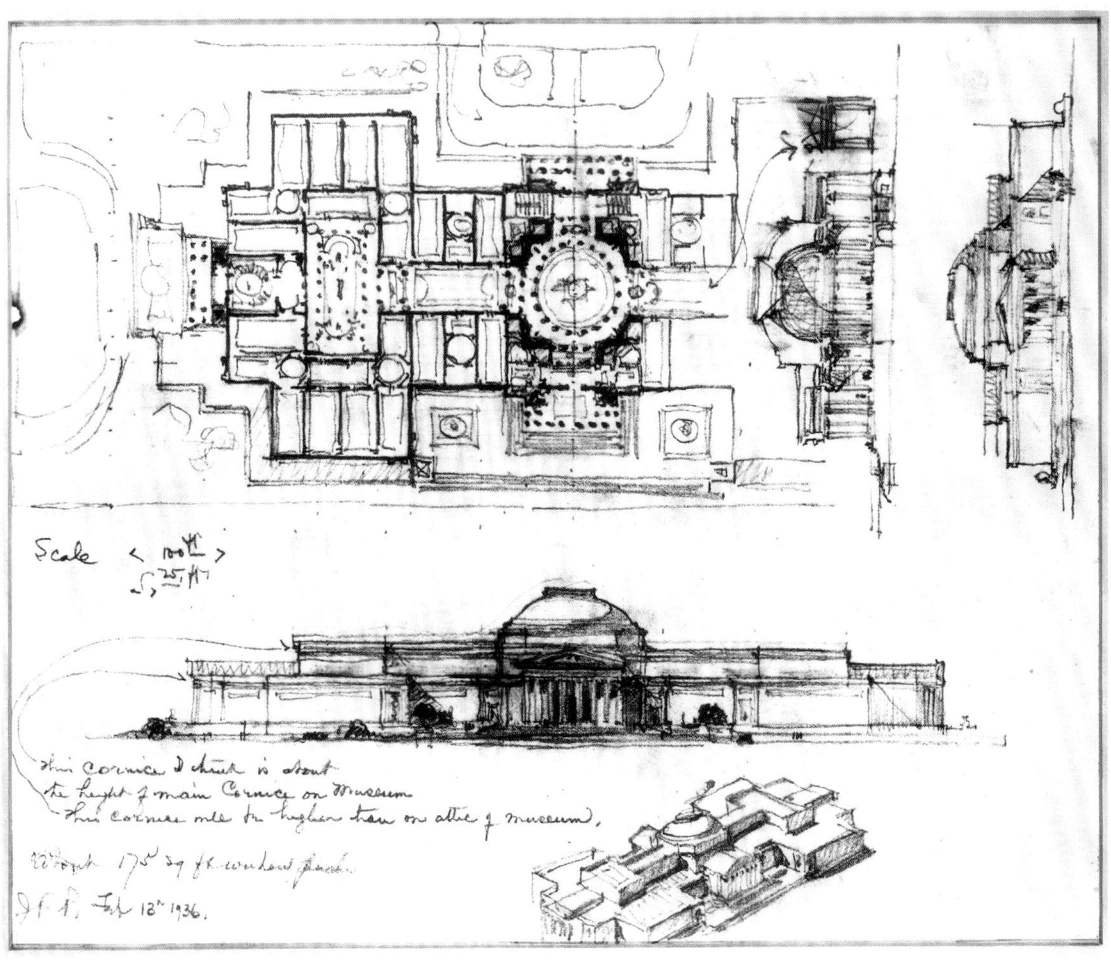
Scale
this Cornice I think is about
the height of main Cornice on Museum
this cornice will be higher than on attic of museum.
J R P Feb 13th 1936.

History

Did you know?
Andrew W. Mellon, an art collector and former secretary of the treasury, commissioned architect John Russell Pope to make the first sketches of the National Gallery of Art. Pope's conceptual drawings, done in February 1936, show a domed structure with symmetrical wings. Inside, galleries for displaying art flank two long halls. Mellon and Pope died within 24 hours of each other in August 1937, shortly after construction of the new museum began.

On March 18, 1941, a new home for art opened to the public within sight of the US Capitol Building: the National Gallery of Art. Since that day when we welcomed our first visitors, millions of people have passed through the majestic bronze doors of our original building. Today, art lovers from around the world explore and enjoy our collections in person and online.

The National Gallery's initial collection consisted of 26 sculptures and 126 paintings, including Raphael's *Alba Madonna*. These works and the funds to construct and maintain the museum were a gift to the nation from philanthropist Andrew W. Mellon. Over the years other generous donors have given exceptional works of European and American art to the National Gallery.

As the museum's permanent holdings grew, it became obvious more space was needed for both the collection and exhibitions. Architect I. M. Pei's design for the East Building added a compelling, modern structure to the National Mall.

With the dedication of the East Building on June 1, 1978, the National Gallery's original structure became known as the West Building. Artworks ranging in date from the 11th to the 19th century are now displayed in its neoclassical galleries. Modern and contemporary art is exhibited in the light-filled Atrium and adjoining spaces of the East Building.

The National Gallery expanded yet again when the six-acre Sculpture Garden to the west opened in 1999. This peaceful outdoor setting provides space for large-scale modern and contemporary sculptures.

Like our ever-diversifying collection, we are continually evolving in how we serve you. In addition to being a leading center for scholarship, education, and cultural programs, we are working to better reflect the nation and its histories through our collection. We not only want to preserve art for future generations, but we also strive to make it more accessible and relevant to the nation today.

Table of Contents

West Building

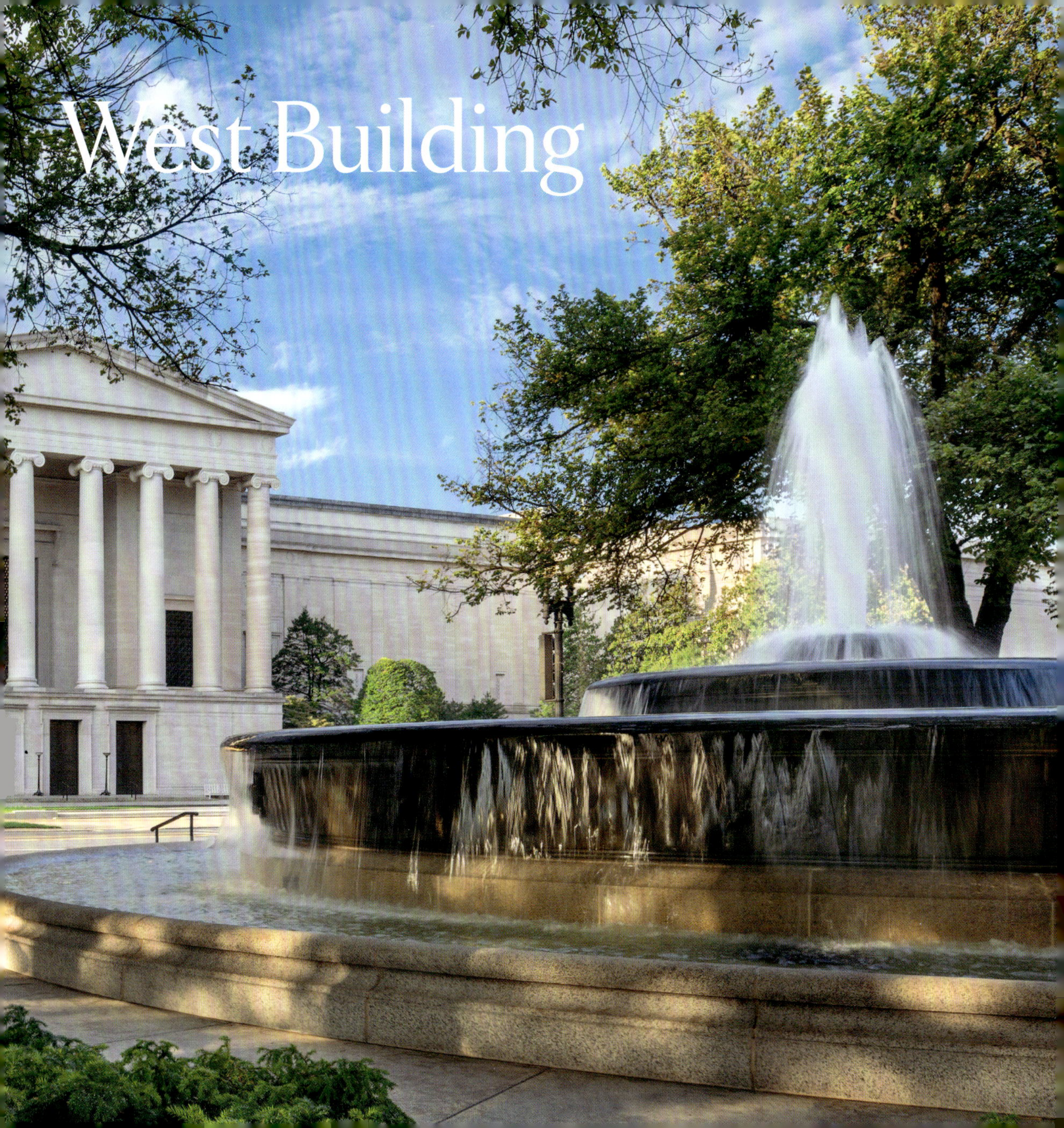

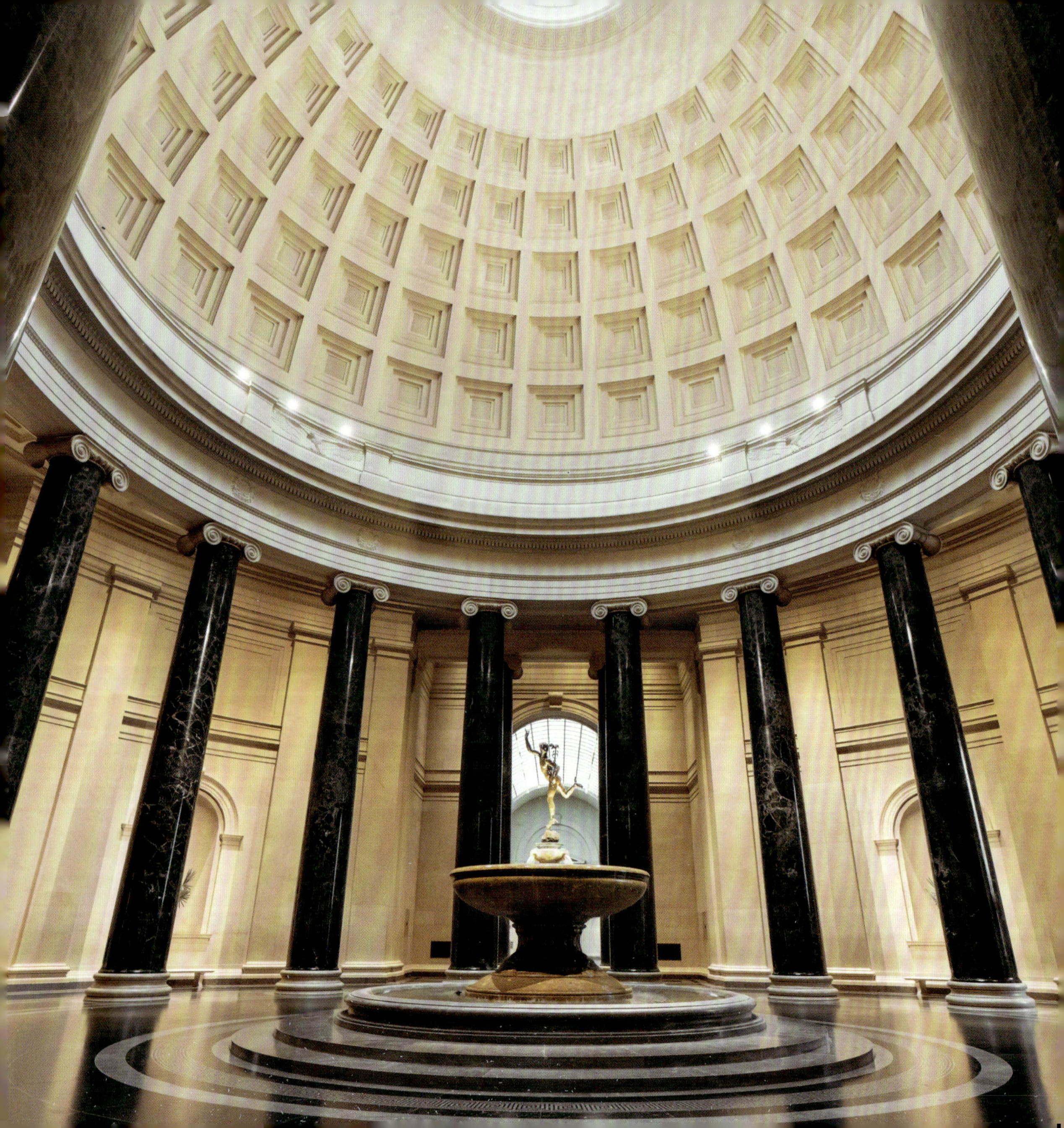

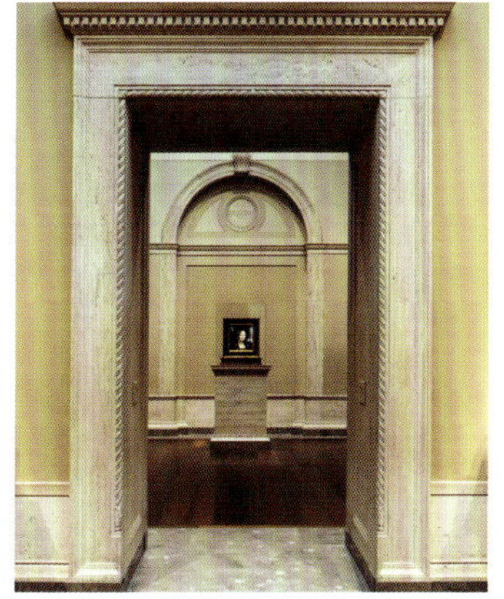

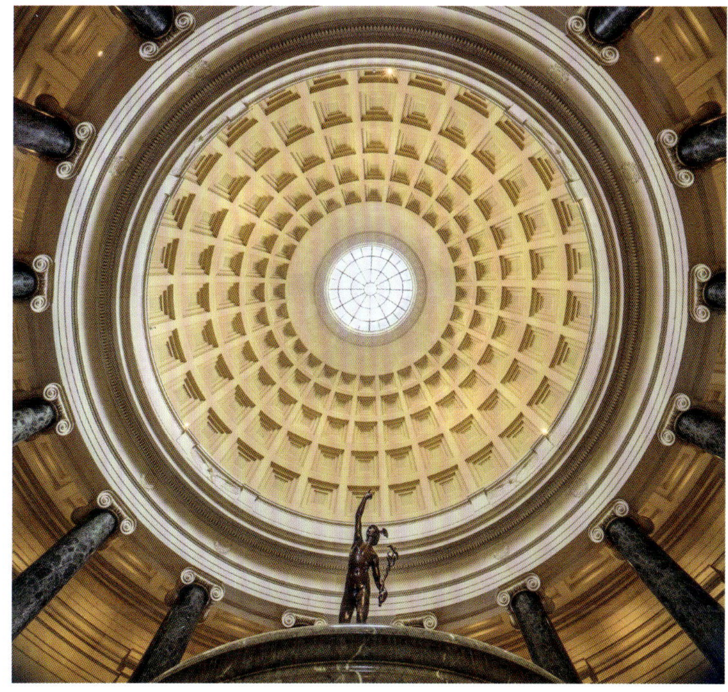

Did you know?
It's 103 feet from the floor of the West Building to the top of the coffered dome. Like the ancient Pantheon in Rome, this rotunda has an oculus at the center to let in light.

Grand marble steps and towering Ionic columns welcome you to the West Building's entrance on the National Mall. Designed in a neoclassical style by architect John Russell Pope, the immense structure might remind you of an ancient Greek temple. The museum's windowless exterior hints at what awaits you inside: walls filled with exceptional works of art.

Inside, the West Building is centered on a colossal domed rotunda. Polished marble columns support the coffered ceiling and add to the sense of grandeur. The rotunda's timeless design and imposing size were inspired by the ancient Pantheon in Rome, Italy. Atop the fountain, a statue of the Roman messenger god Mercury balances on one foot, as if caught mid-stride (left). Extending from this central fountain are two long hallways with barrel-vaulted ceilings. The three-acre roof is covered almost entirely by skylights, allowing natural light to filter into the spaces below.

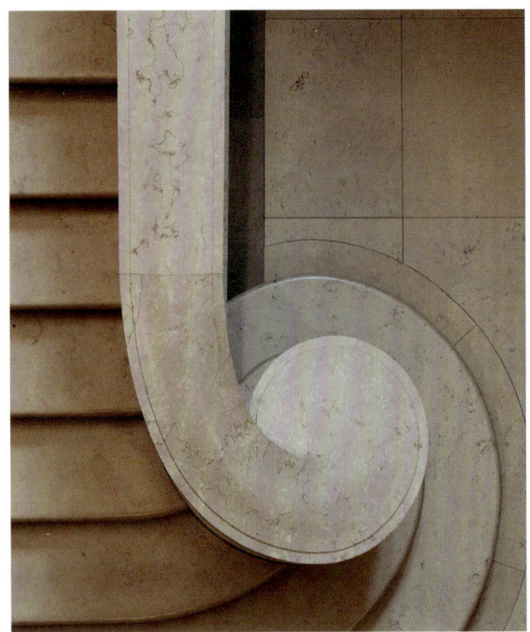

Did you know?
Tiny fossils of shelled creatures are embedded in the marble of the floors, walls, stairways, and even some of the restroom wall panels throughout the West Building.

Did you also know?
Glass pyramids designed by architect I. M. Pei decorate the plaza that connects the West Building (right) and the East Building.

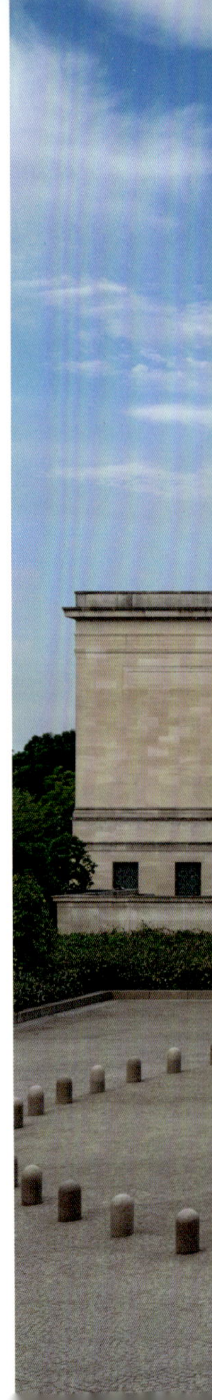

Artworks within these main floor galleries are arranged by time and geography. You might choose to focus on a certain era or prefer to wander through the centuries. Works on view range from religious scenes from the Byzantine period to the Middle Ages and on to the Italian Renaissance. Intimate genre scenes by Johannes Vermeer, portraits by Rembrandt van Rijn, and detailed Dutch still lifes stand out among our many paintings from northern Europe. Portraits and breathtaking landscapes set in Italy, England, or North America are displayed across the hall from colorful paintings created by the French impressionists.

More of the National Gallery's vast collection is on view in the ground floor galleries. There, you can see decorative arts in addition to sculptures by French artists Auguste Rodin and Edgar Degas. In nearby galleries are exhibitions of photographs as well as prints, drawings, and other works on paper.

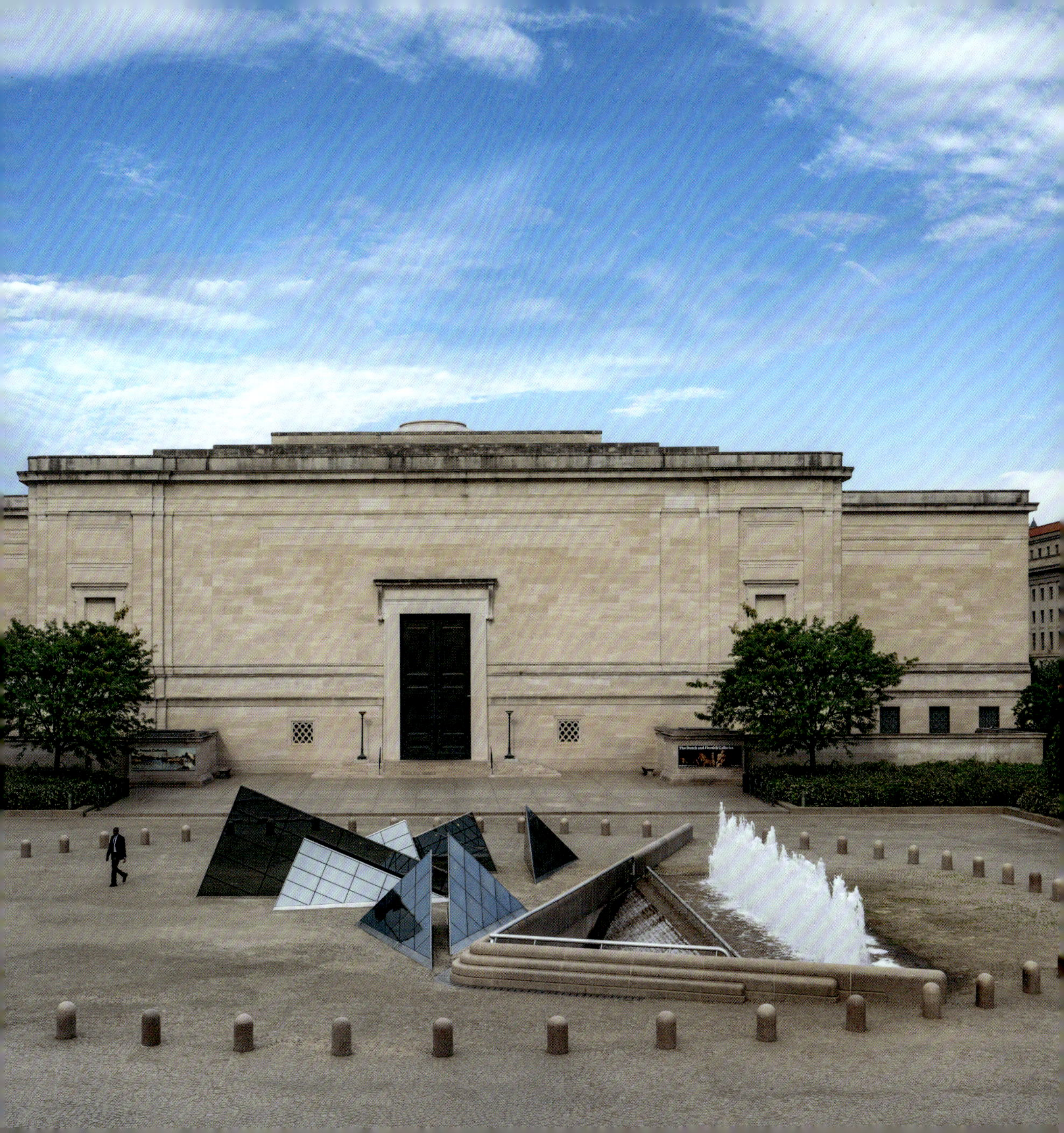

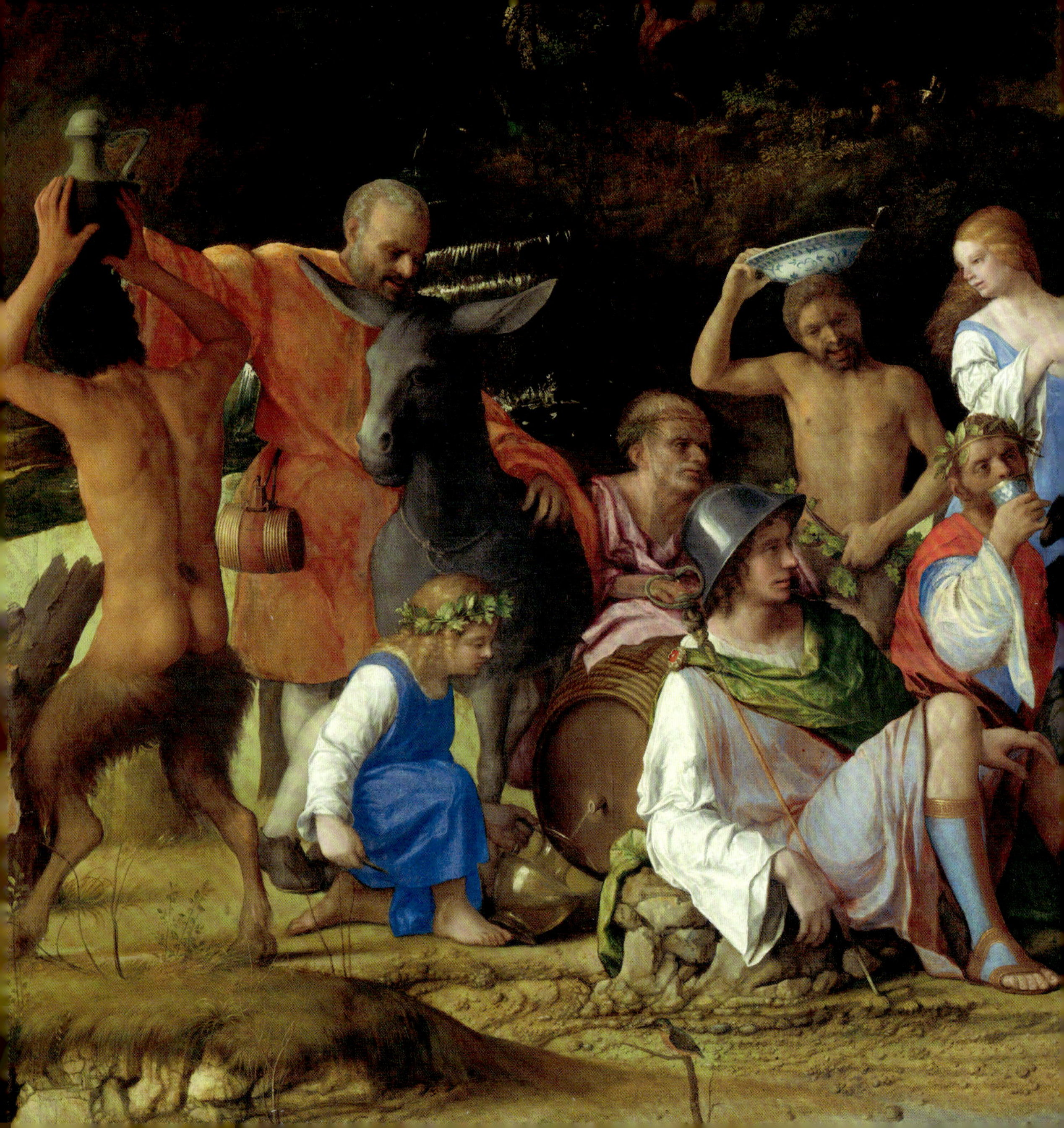

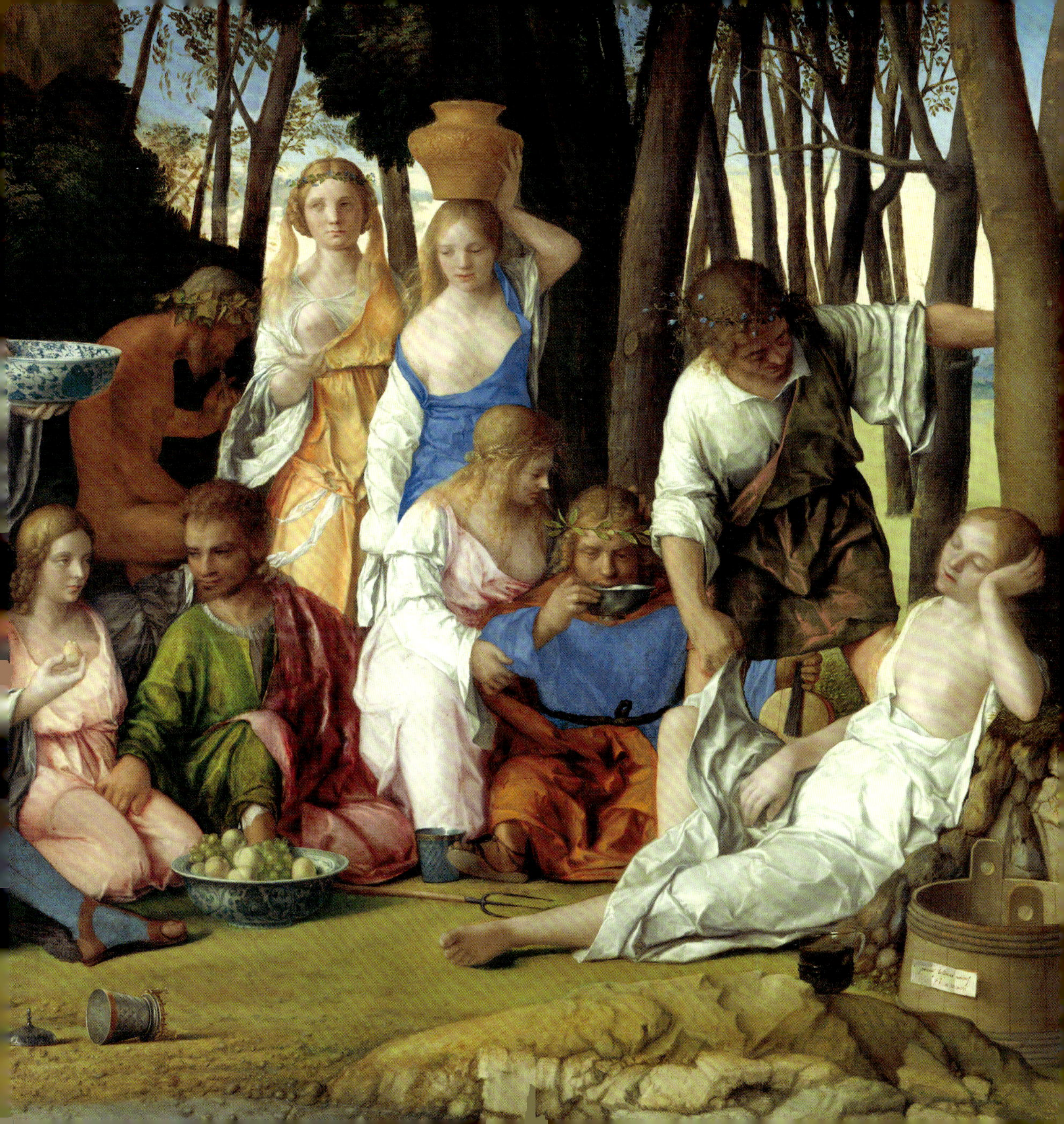

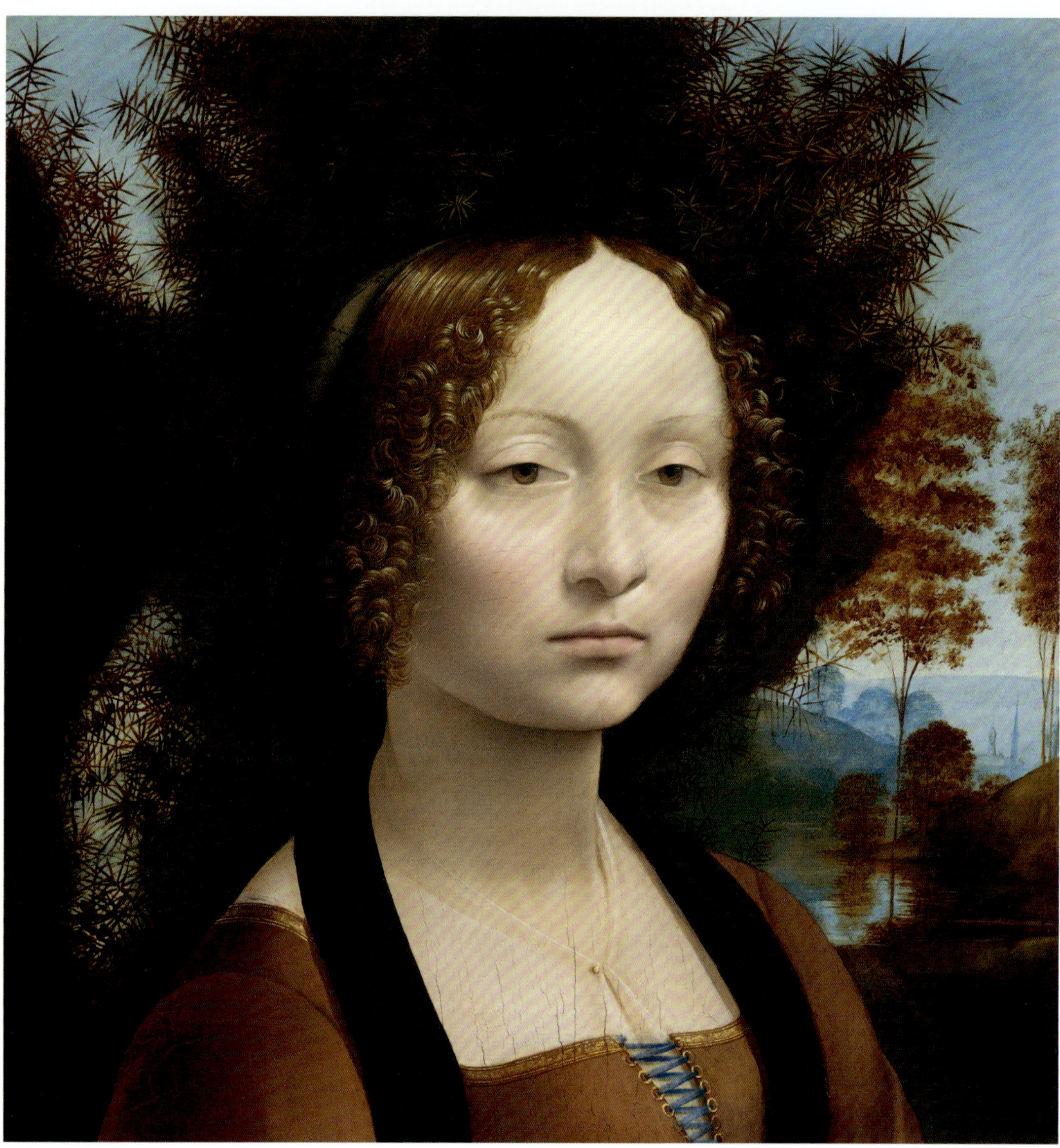

Leonardo da Vinci
Florentine, 1452–1519

Ginevra de' Benci
c. 1474/1478

oil on panel

AILSA MELLON BRUCE FUND
1967.6.1.A

It is impossible to guess what 16-year-old Ginevra de' Benci was thinking as she sat for this portrait to commemorate her upcoming marriage. The young Florentine woman has a distant gaze. Her flawless skin and shining curls are offset by a halo of juniper leaves, a reference to her name, Ginevra. This treasured work, which is the only painting by Leonardo da Vinci in the Americas, reveals the artist's mastery of the paint medium. Note the subtle shading of Ginevra's face, the tiny spires on the horizon, and the detailed foliage on both sides of the panel.

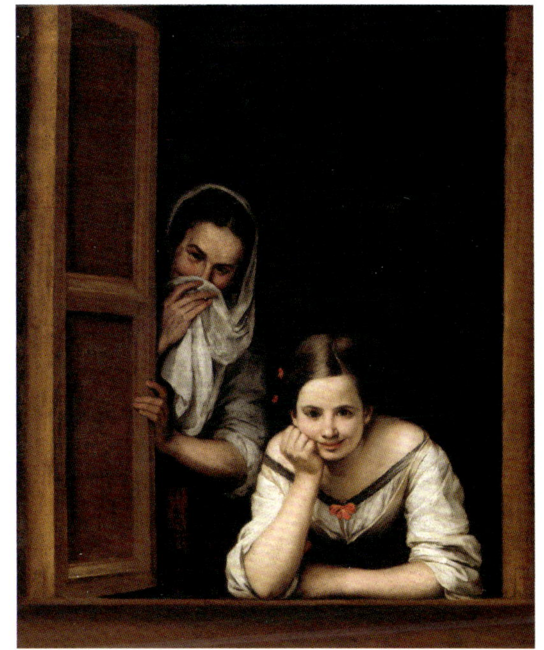

Bartolomé Esteban Murillo
Spanish, 1617–1682

Two Women at a Window
c. 1655/1660

oil on canvas

WIDENER COLLECTION
1942.9.46

What is so captivating to the woman leaning intently over the windowsill? And what is so amusing to her companion, who stifles a laugh with her shawl? Are they looking at us? Our attention might suddenly feel inappropriate. The painting hints at female modesty and propriety. These 17th-century Spanish women were meant to be protected and sheltered. By boldly opening a window onto their lives, artist Bartolomé Esteban Murillo pulls back restrictive shutters on the world of women.

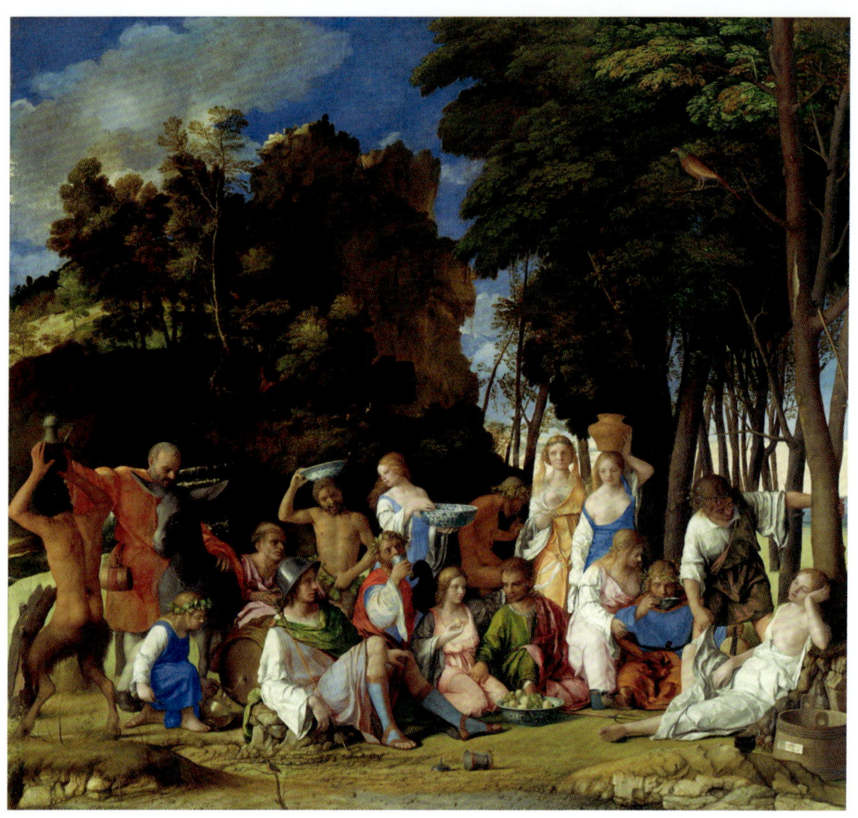

Giovanni Bellini
Venetian, c. 1430/1435–1516

Titian
Venetian, 1488/1490–1576

The Feast of the Gods
1514/1529

oil on canvas

WIDENER COLLECTION
1942.9.1

No one parties like the gods—at least not like the mythological ones in this painting, a collaboration by the Renaissance artists Giovanni Bellini and Titian. The picture was the first in a series of bacchanals commissioned by Duke Alfonso d'Este to decorate the *camerino d'alabastro* (alabaster study) of his castle in Ferrara. It's based on a scene from Ovid's *Fasti*, a poem in Latin. At this banquet, Jupiter, Neptune, and Apollo feast in the woods as nymphs and satyrs attend to their every desire. Priapus, the god of fertility, inappropriately lifts the dress of the sleeping nymph Lotis. Dark trees provide both privacy to the scandalous affair and depth to the composition.

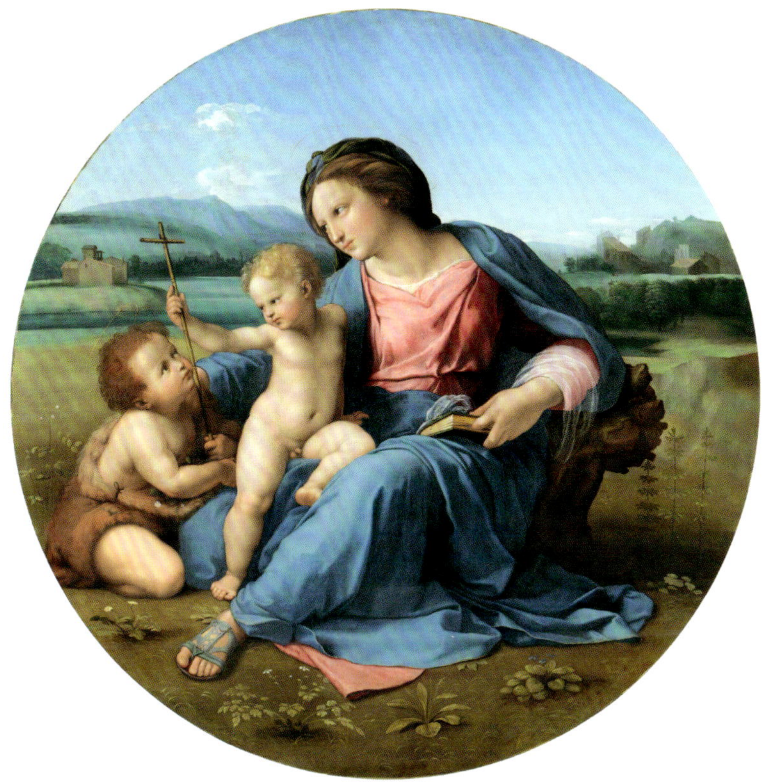

Raphael
Marchigian, 1483–1520

The Alba Madonna
c. 1510

oil on panel transferred to canvas

ANDREW W. MELLON COLLECTION
1937.1.24

Renaissance artist Raphael was famous in his own time. It is easy to understand why. His images are vibrant, emotional, and flawless in execution. In this round-format religious painting, called a tondo, Mary and a young John the Baptist lean in toward Jesus. Their gazes fall on the child as he receives the burden of the cross on which he will be crucified to pay for the wrongs of others. The intense moment is softened by the lush green landscape and the pale pinks and blues of Mary's draped garment. Seated on the bare ground, the humble Madonna accepts her son's fate.

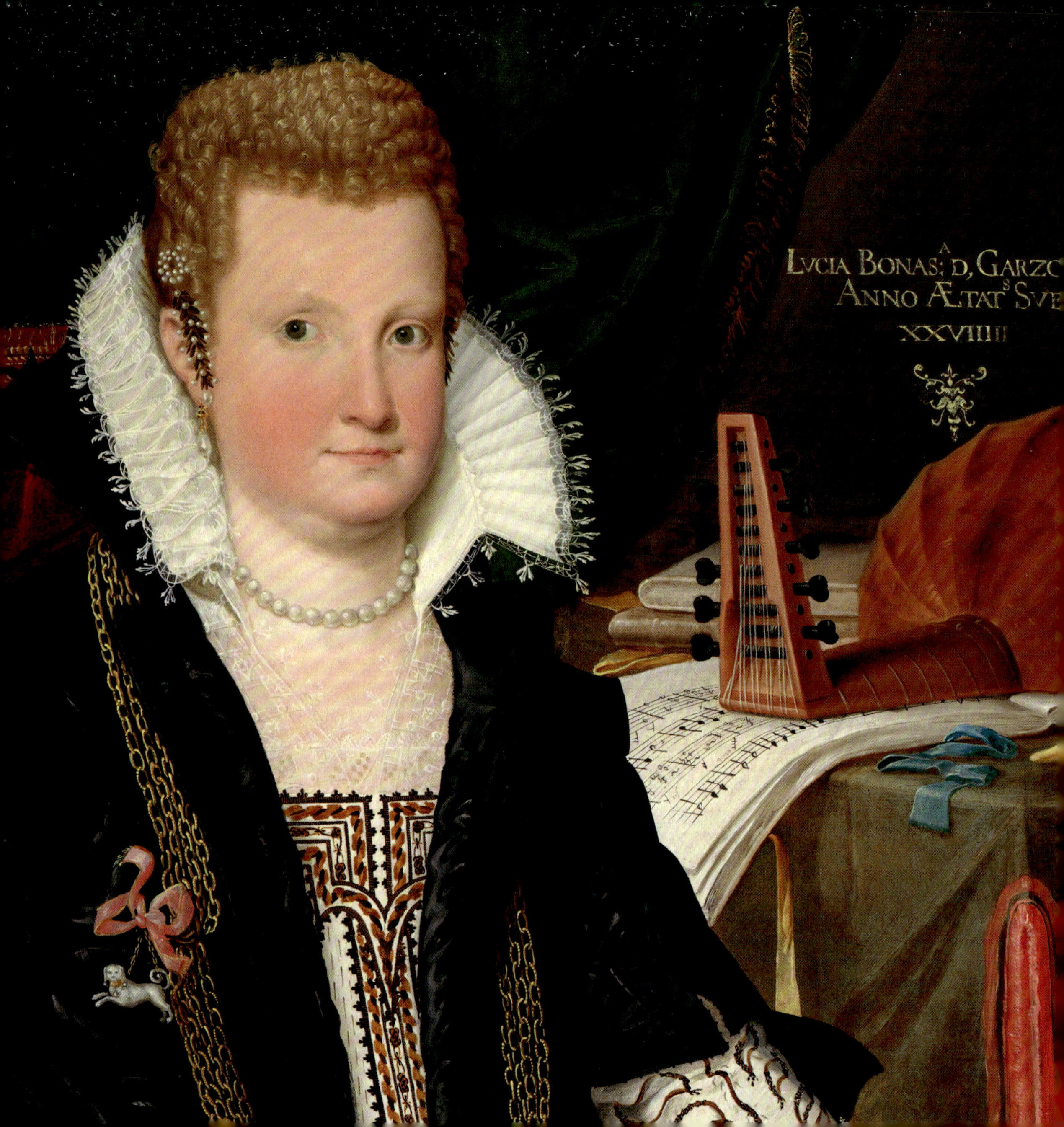
LVCIA BONAS: A D, GARZO
ANNO ÆTAT S SVE
XXVIIII

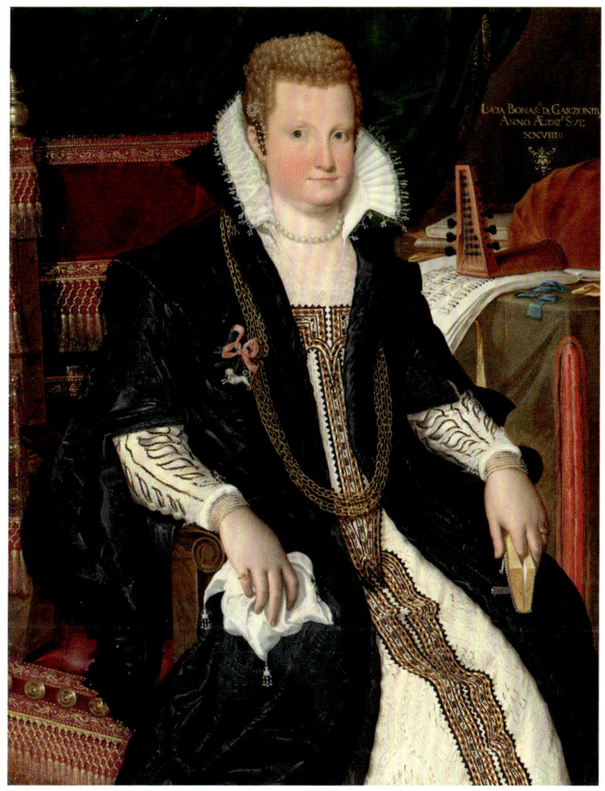

Lavinia Fontana
Italian, 1552–1614

Lucia Bonasoni Garzoni
c. 1590

oil on canvas

GIFT OF FUNDS FROM ANONYMOUS IN MEMORY OF MONTANA WALKER STRAUSS, AND PATRONS' PERMANENT FUND
2022.38.1

Lucia Bonasoni Garzoni, perfectly coiffed and magnificently dressed, stares at us intently. A lute and sheet music on the table beside her declare her skill as a musician. The accomplished 16th-century noblewoman was highly regarded for her musical talents at a time when few women gained widespread recognition. The painter was also a woman, another rarity in the 1500s. What did sitter and artist talk about as Garzoni posed for Lavinia Fontana? The challenges of being an accomplished woman in a man's world? Perhaps they let this powerful portrait speak for itself.

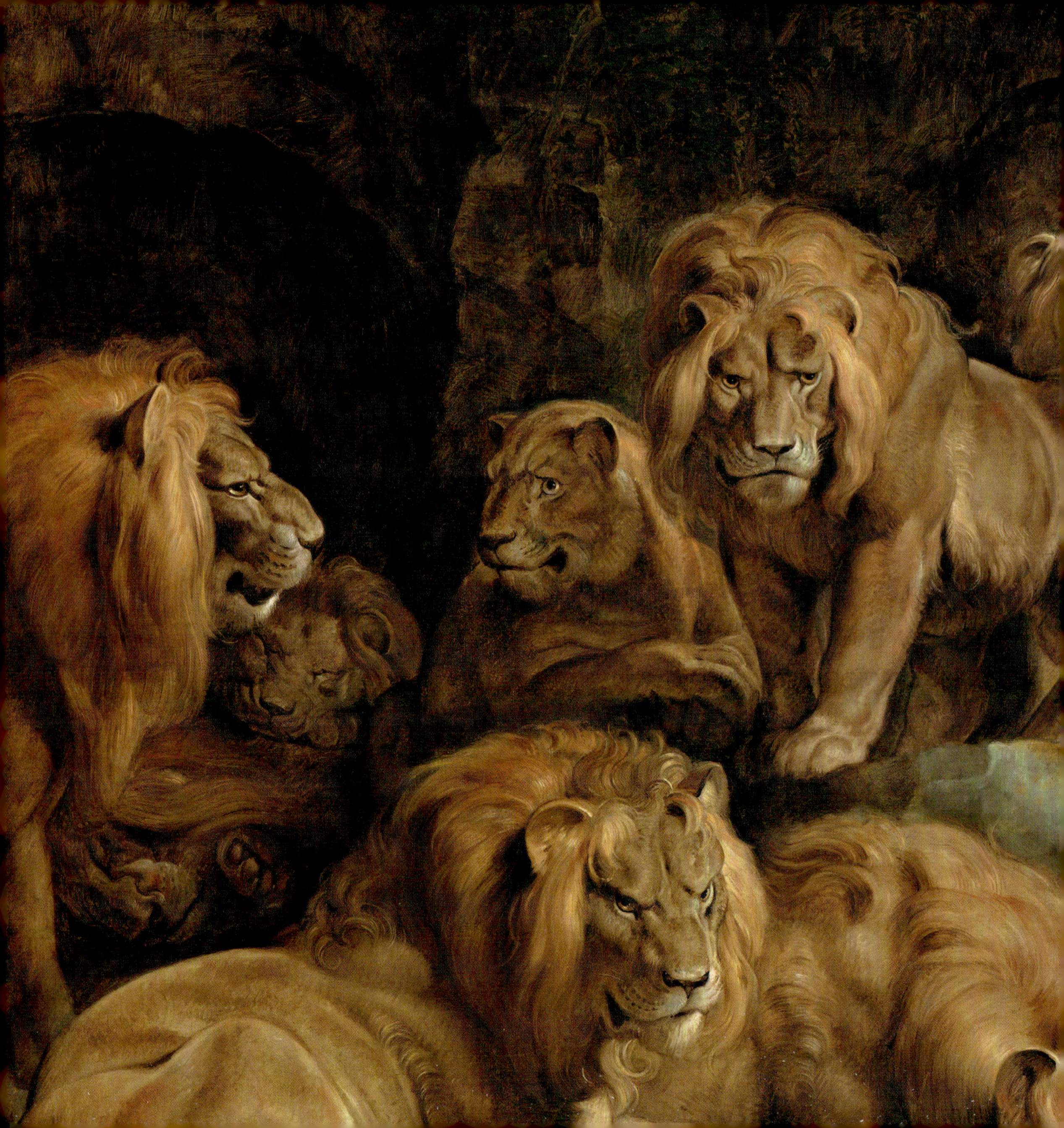

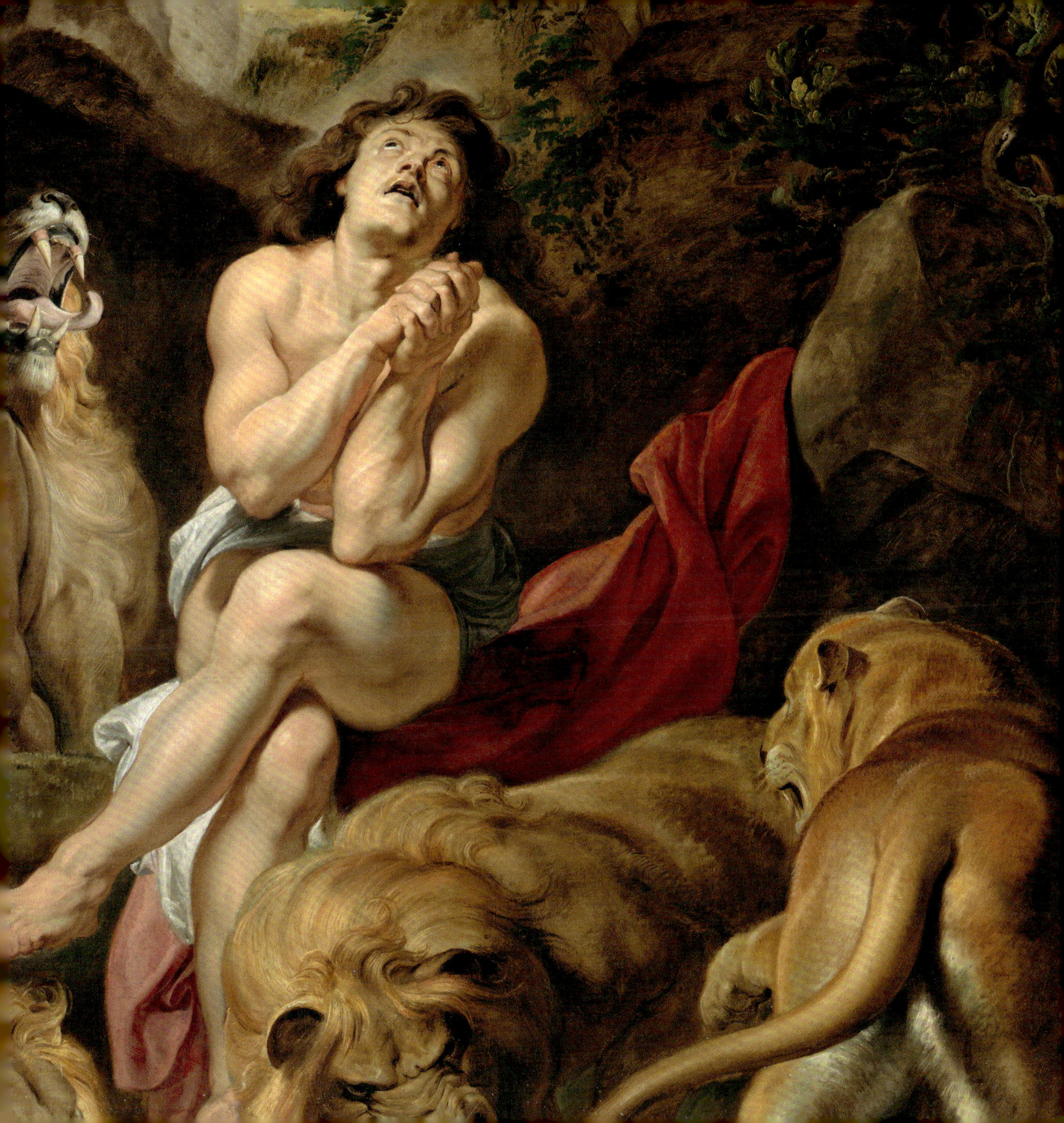

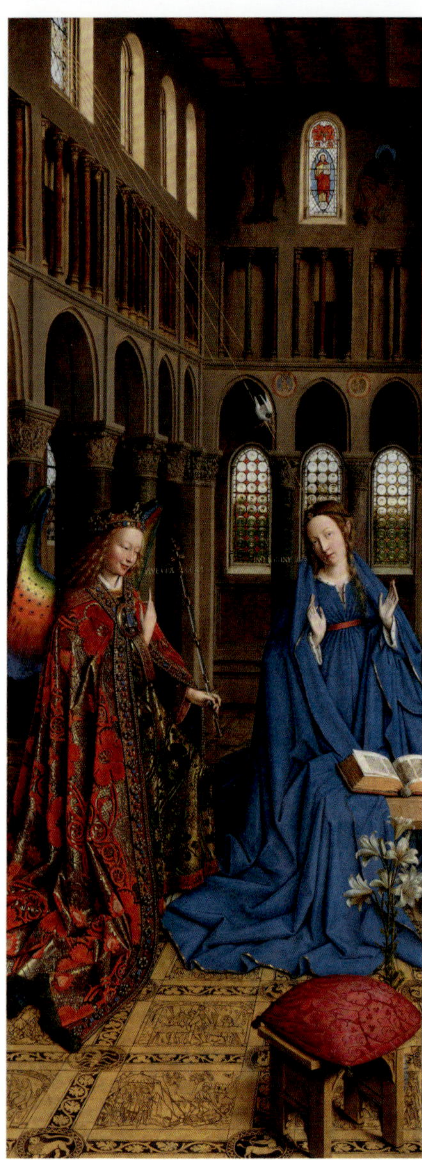

Jan van Eyck
Netherlandish, c. 1390–1441

The Annunciation
c. 1434/1436

oil on canvas transferred from panel

ANDREW W. MELLON COLLECTION
1937.1.39

A play and a painting appear to have merged in Jan van Eyck's dramatic *Annunciation*, which is rich with Christian symbolism. The rainbow-winged archangel Gabriel tells the Virgin Mary that God has chosen her to bear his son. This message is revealed in gold letters near the angel's mouth. Mary throws up her hands in surprise but accepts her fate. Her reply is noted in a golden phrase, written in reverse for God to see from above. This divine scene is set in a church, with every arch, window, and column finely rendered in detail.

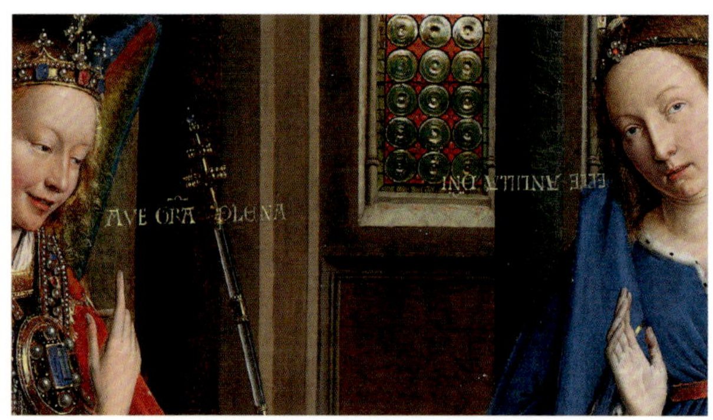

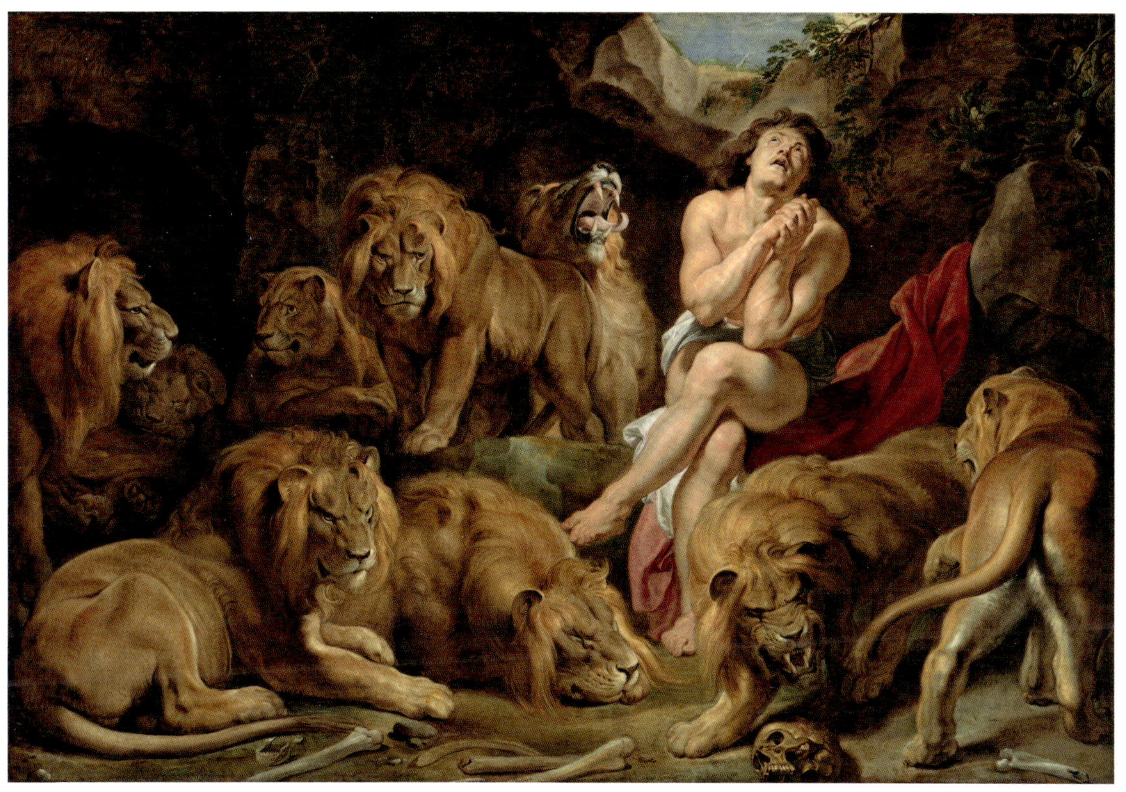

Sir Peter Paul Rubens
Flemish, 1577–1640

Daniel in the Lions' Den
c. 1614/1616

oil on canvas

AILSA MELLON BRUCE FUND
1965.13.1

Peter Paul Rubens's enormous painting, based on the biblical story of Daniel, puts us right in the lions' den. The Jewish youth was condemned to spend the night with the brutal beasts for worshipping his God rather than the Persian king Darius. Will he survive? The pacing animals might attack the frantically praying Daniel at any minute. Their realistic fur makes our own hair stand on end. We can only hope that the light encircling Daniel ensures his safety—and miraculously, it does. This story of faith, theatrically portrayed at such a grand scale, was meant to encourage passion and piety.

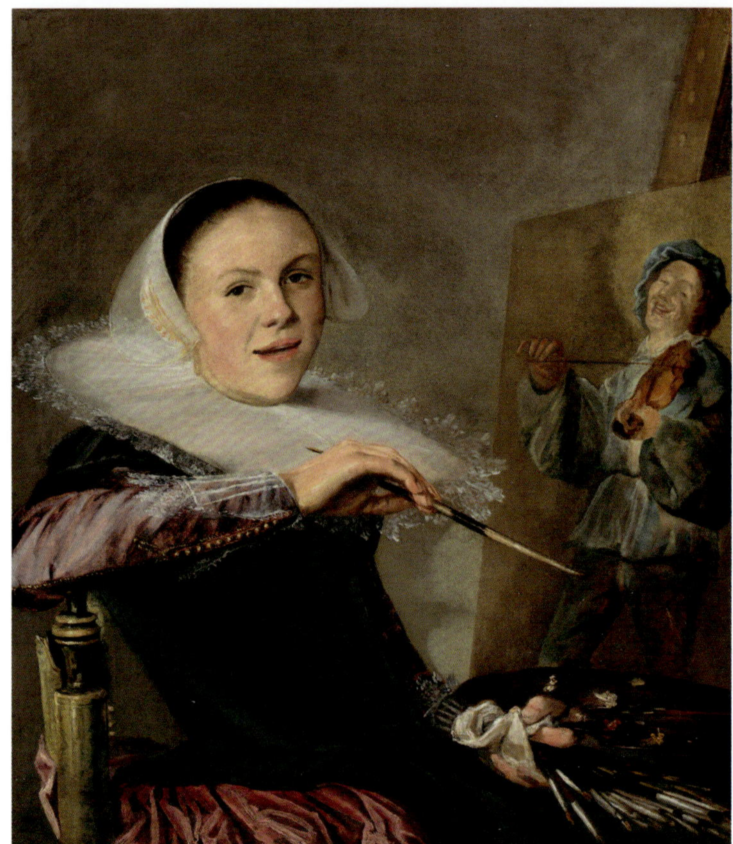

Judith Leyster
Dutch, 1609–1660

Self-Portrait
c. 1630

oil on canvas

GIFT OF MR. AND MRS. ROBERT WOODS BLISS
1949.6.1

Here is Dutch artist Judith Leyster at her easel, taking a break from painting to engage with us. In what might be considered an early selfie, she leans her forearm on the chair and suspends her paintbrush in midair, as if she'll turn back to the canvas in a moment. Leyster, recognized as a master artist in the Saint Luke's Guild of Haarlem, was publicly praised for her work. This was a rare accomplishment for a woman in 17th-century Holland. She wields the tools of her trade—a palette and no fewer than 18 paintbrushes—with confidence and joy.

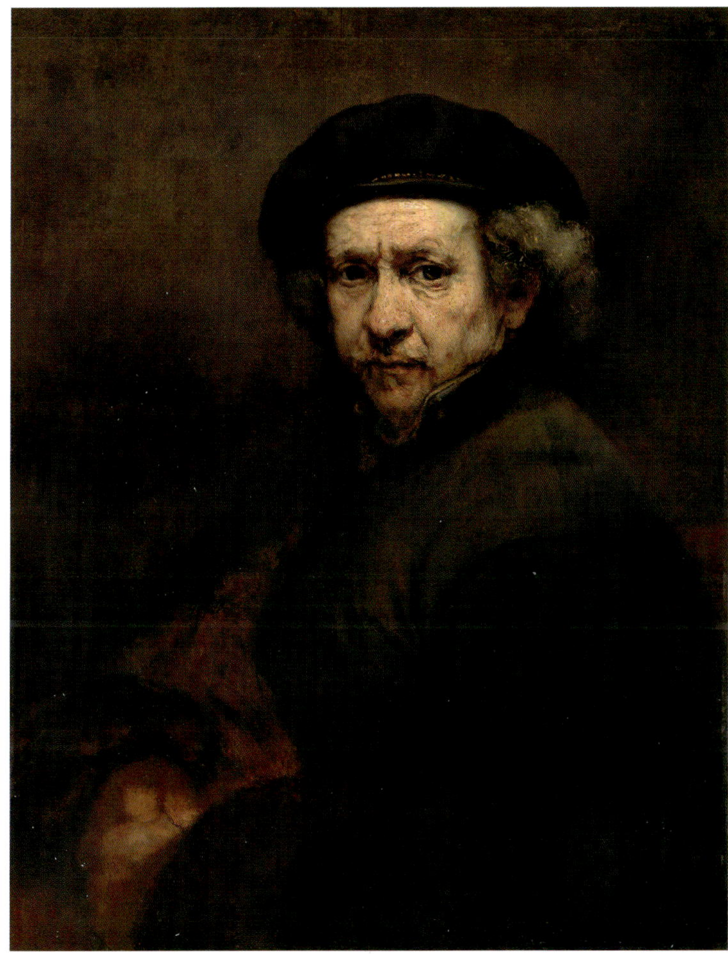

Rembrandt van Rijn
Dutch, 1606–1669

Self-Portrait
1659

oil on canvas

ANDREW W. MELLON COLLECTION
1937.1.72

The man's surroundings are blurred, but his illuminated face is finely detailed. The sad eyes fix on us intently. What is he trying to communicate? We know he is Rembrandt van Rijn, a Dutch painter of extraordinary fame today, but he seems unsettled. His brows are knitted, his cheeks are sunken, and deep wrinkles gather at his forehead and eyes. Painted when the artist was 53 years old, this penetrating work was made after Rembrandt was forced to sell his possessions to pay off creditors. They could not take away his skill or dignity, which he displays in this self-portrait.

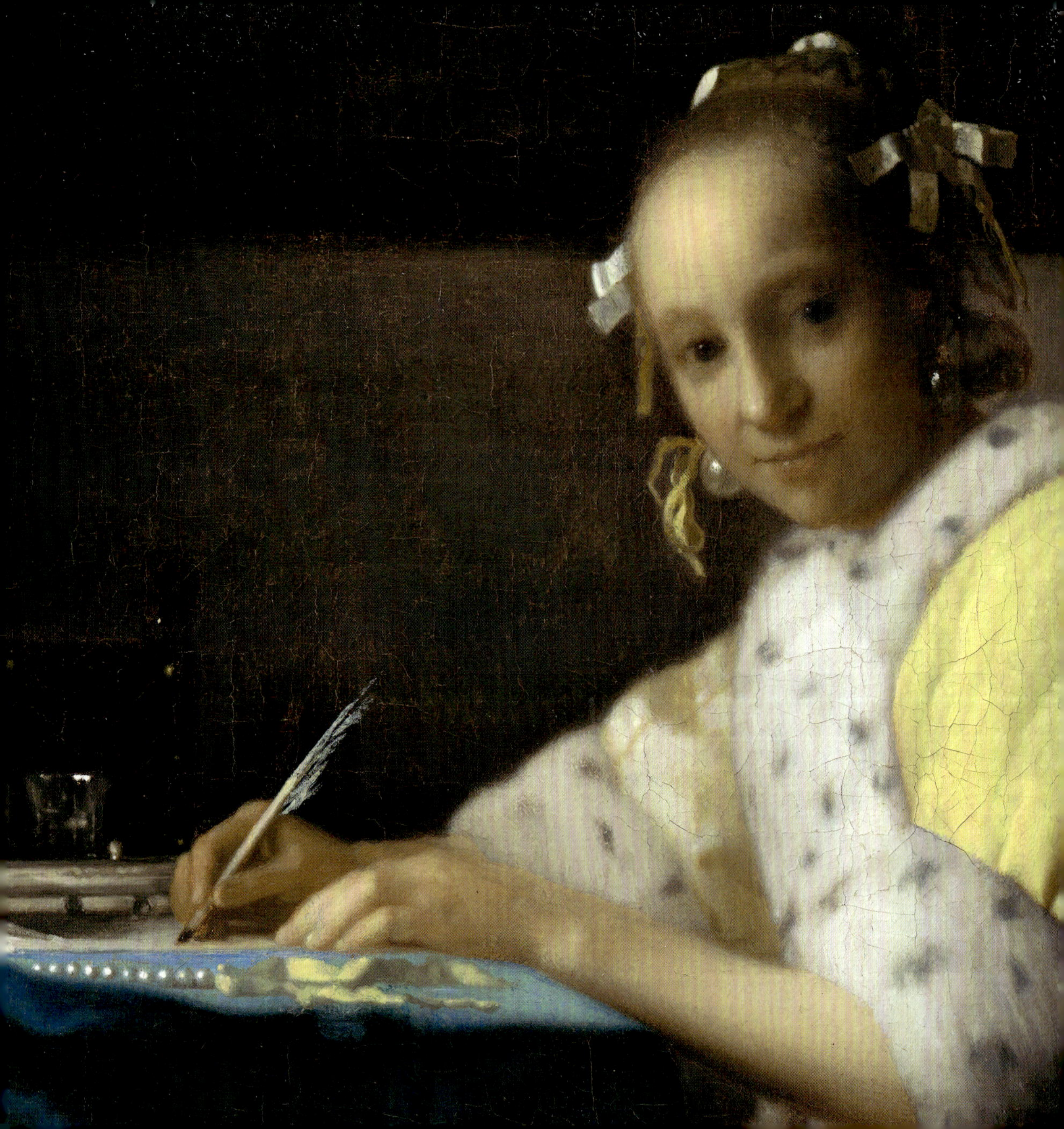

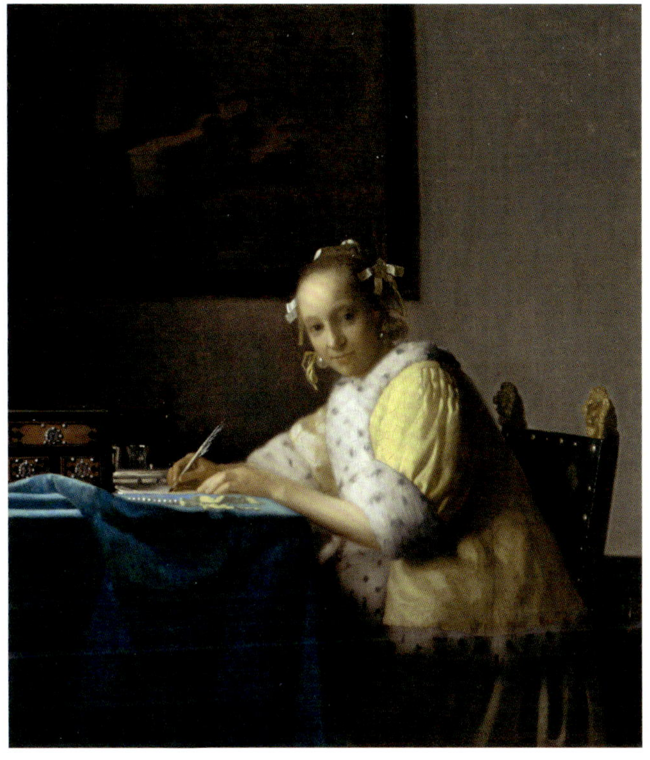

Johannes Vermeer
Dutch, 1632–1675

A Lady Writing
c. 1665

oil on canvas

GIFT OF HARRY WALDRON HAVEMEYER AND HORACE HAVEMEYER, JR., IN MEMORY OF THEIR FATHER, HORACE HAVEMEYER
1962.10.1

It doesn't matter what this elegantly dressed lady is writing as she sits at her desk, perhaps before a window. Johannes Vermeer uses soft, natural light to illuminate the table, her face, and the front of her buttery yellow jacket. Her pearls and bows gleam. As her body inclines toward her work, her gaze meets ours. This is not simply a portrait of a woman performing a mundane task. Through his extraordinary skill, Vermeer heightens an intimate moment and gives it importance. Though we don't know her name, this lady embodies a vision of the intelligence and charm of privileged Dutch women of her time.

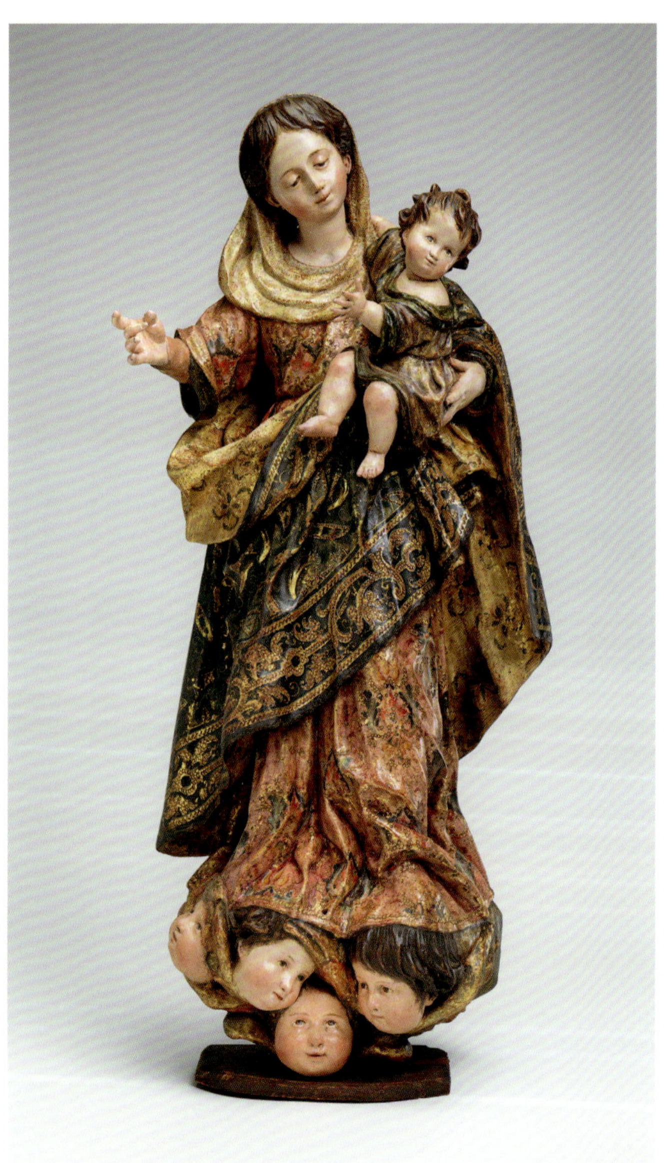

Luisa Roldán
Spanish, 1650–1704

Virgin and Child
c. 1680/1686

painted wood

PEPITA MILMORE MEMORIAL FUND, PATRONS' PERMANENT FUND AND WILLIAM AND BUFFY CAFRITZ FAMILY SCULPTURE FUND
2022.39.1

Spanish women artists of the 17th century worked anonymously. They were not publicly acknowledged, and today we rarely know their names. Luisa Roldán—later called La Roldana—is an exception. She learned her trade from her father, a noted sculptor in Seville, and established her own workshop in Cádiz. Later, she served as court sculptor to King Carlos II and his successor, Felipe V, in Madrid. Her hard-won recognition for her work did not guarantee financial success: Roldán died in poverty.

Hiram Powers
American, 1805–1873

The Greek Slave
model 1841–1843, carved 1846

Seravezza marble

CORCORAN COLLECTION
(GIFT OF WILLIAM WILSON CORCORAN, 1873)
2014.79.37

Sensational and scandalous for an American audience unused to seeing classically nude statues of women, this figure by Hiram Powers caused a frenzy when it was first exhibited in the mid-19th century. Curious viewers came in droves to see it after Powers sent several copies from Italy, where he created the work. His sculpture was inspired by Greece's struggle for independence in the 1820s, but American abolitionists seized on it as a condemnation of slavery. The controversial artwork soon became America's most famous sculpture. Powers made numerous reproductions, and the image graced everyday items, from sheet music to tobacco tins.

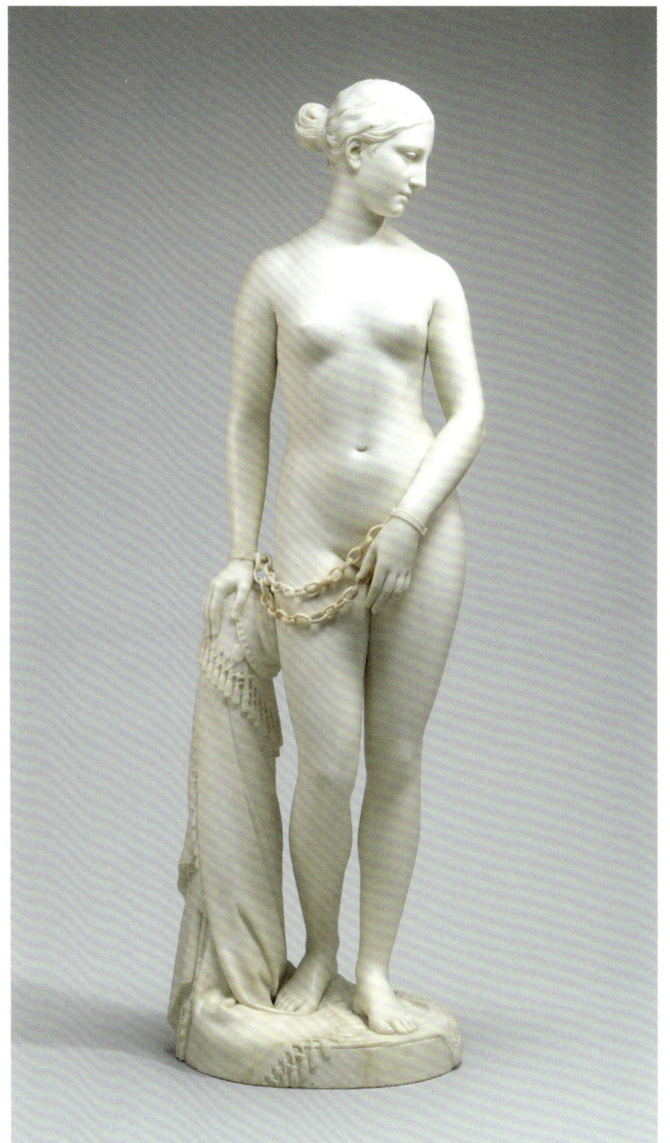

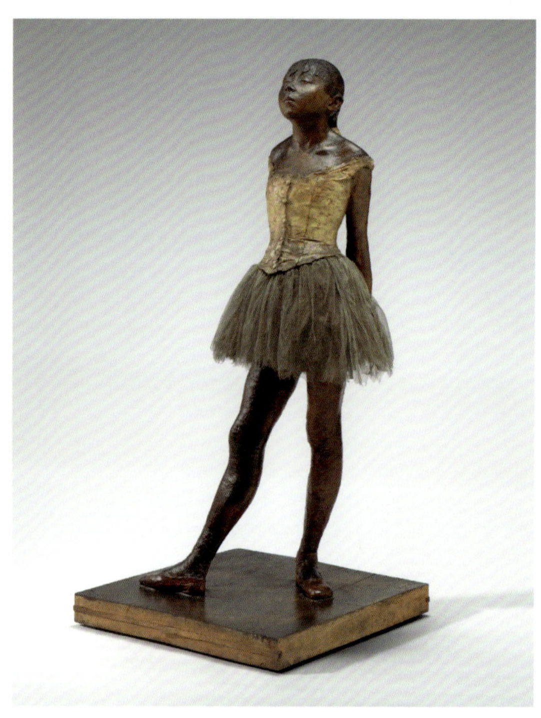

Edgar Degas
French, 1834–1917

Little Dancer Aged Fourteen
1878–1881

pigmented beeswax, clay, metal armature, rope, paintbrushes, human hair, silk and linen ribbon, cotton faille bodice, cotton and silk tutu, linen slippers, on wooden base

COLLECTION OF MR. AND MRS. PAUL MELLON
1999.80.28

Edgar Degas's *Little Dancer Aged Fourteen* provoked controversy when it was exhibited in Paris in 1881. It was too real! Viewers who were used to seeing idealized subjects in artworks did not know how to react to this young ballerina in a tutu, bodice, slippers, and hair ribbon. Degas's young model for this work was Marie van Goethem, a student at the Paris Opera Ballet school and the daughter of working-class parents. Poor teenage ballerinas of that time, who worked to supplement their families' incomes, were often subject to unwanted attention from men. By presenting the *Little Dancer* as a lifelike and dignified person, Degas shows compassion for her plight.

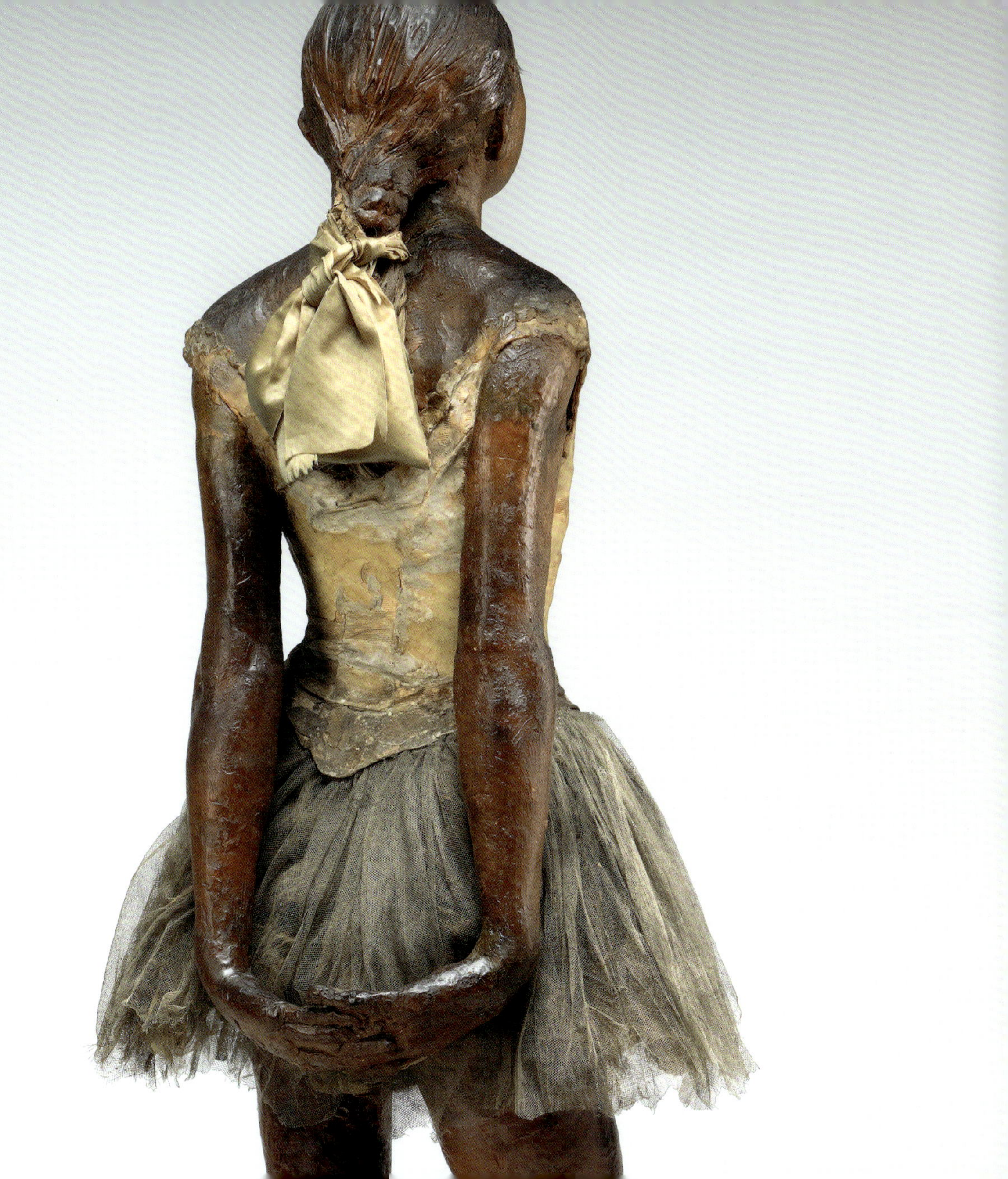

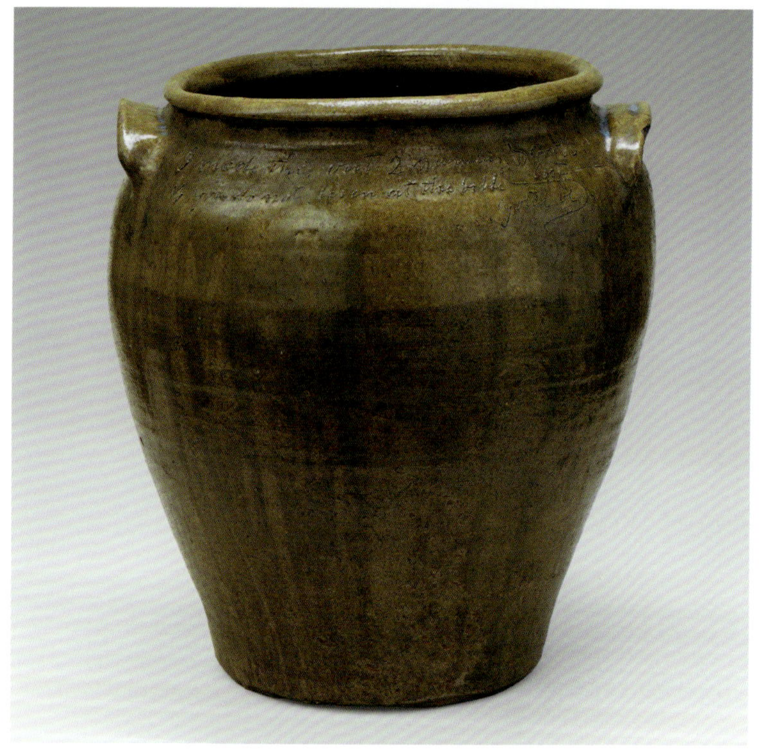

David Drake
American, c. 1801–1870s

Storage Jar
1859

alkaline-glazed stoneware

ANONYMOUS GIFT OF FUNDS
2023.2.1

This graceful jar is simple in design, beautiful in execution, and prominently signed *Dave* by its creator. Such a bold claim to authorship might not seem unusual to us today. After all, the object shows incredible skill, and the potter should be justly proud. We should note, however, that this storage vessel was made by an enslaved Black man at a ceramics manufactory in South Carolina in 1859. It was crafted during a time when it was unlawful to teach enslaved workers to read and write. Dave took risks to announce his identity as he practiced his art.

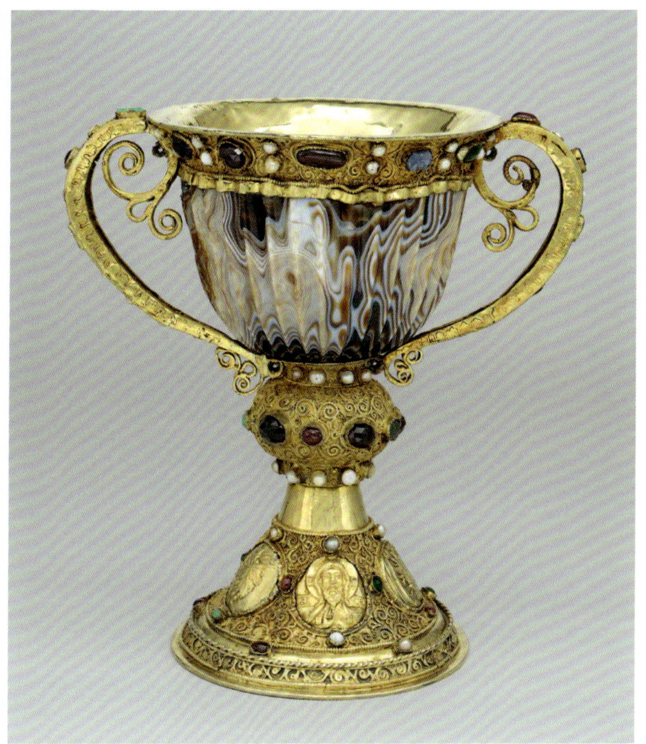

French, mid-12th century (mounting); Alexandrian, 2nd/1st century BCE (cup)

Chalice of the Abbot Suger of Saint-Denis

sardonyx cup with heavily gilded silver mounting, adorned with filigrees set with stones, pearls, glass insets, and opaque white glass pearls

WIDENER COLLECTION
1942.9.277

Works of art are subject to continual change and movement. This chalice, made of materials from around the world, has been altered several times during the 2,000 years of its history. The oldest part is the cup, which was carved in ancient Egypt. Around 1137/1140, Abbot Suger ordered goldsmiths to create the gem-studded metalwork. This process transformed the cup into a chalice for the royal Catholic church of Saint-Denis near Paris. The chalice remained in use there until 1791, when it was removed during the French Revolution. Its appearance changed again as later owners passed it from France to England and finally to the United States.

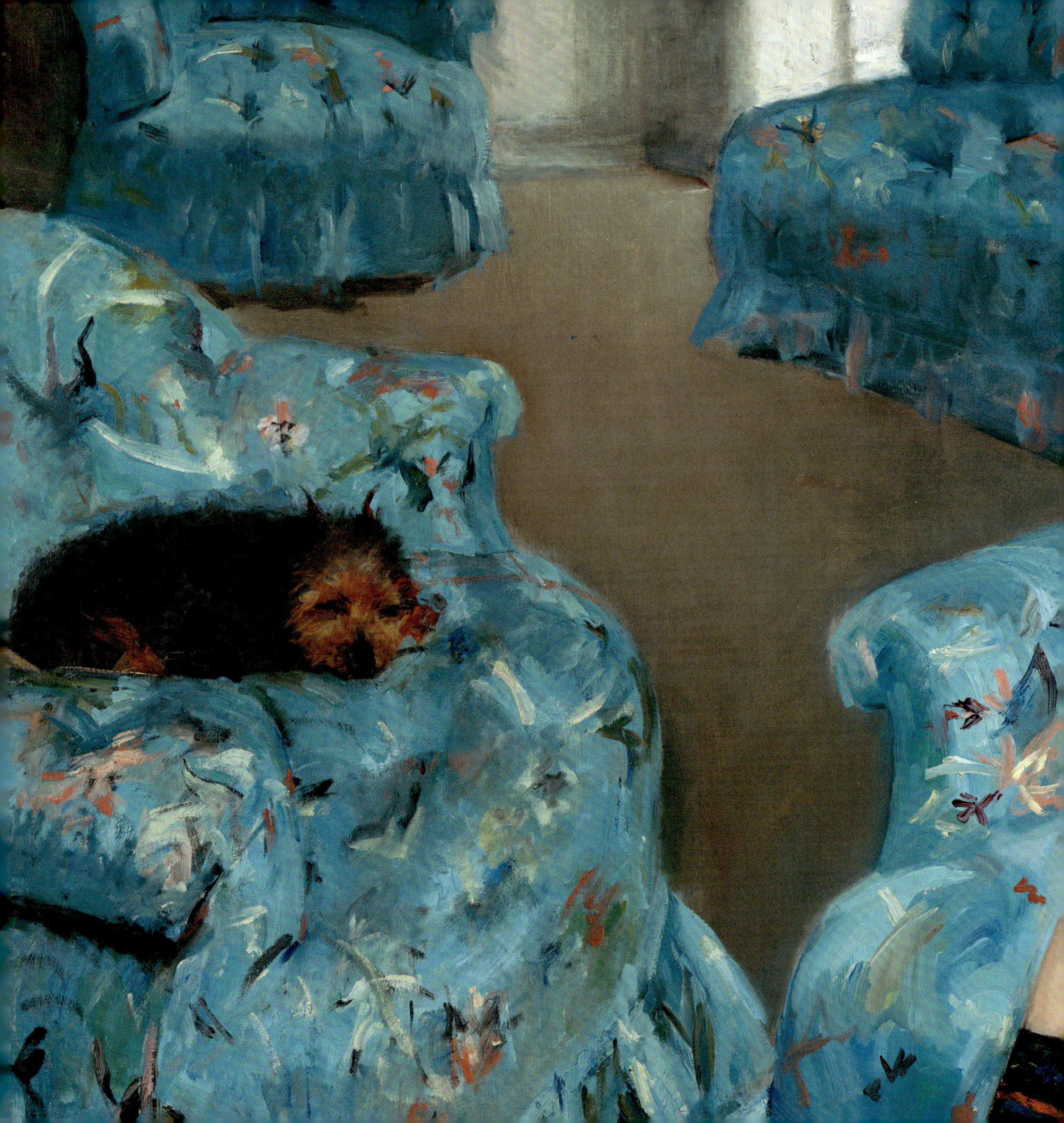

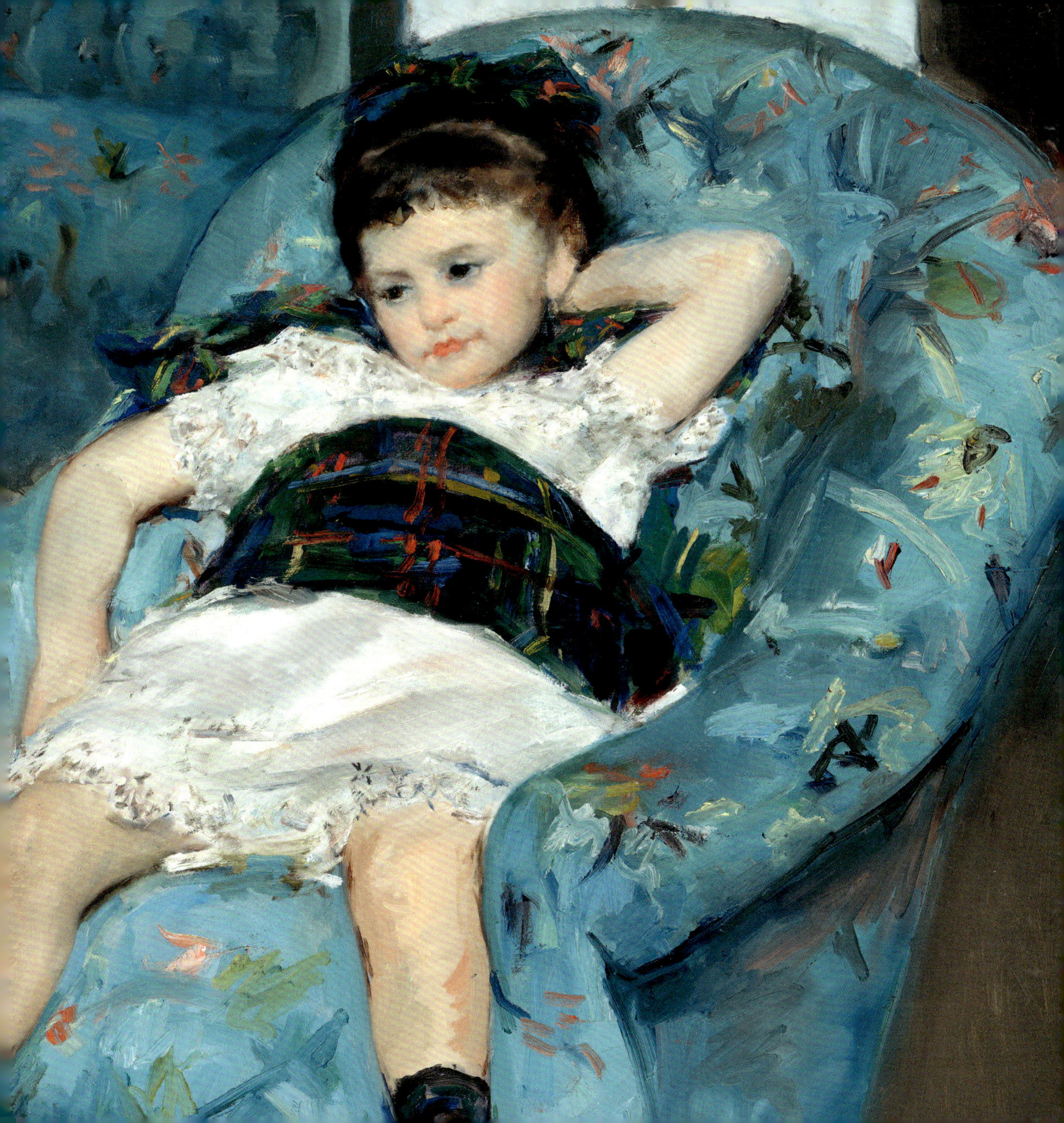

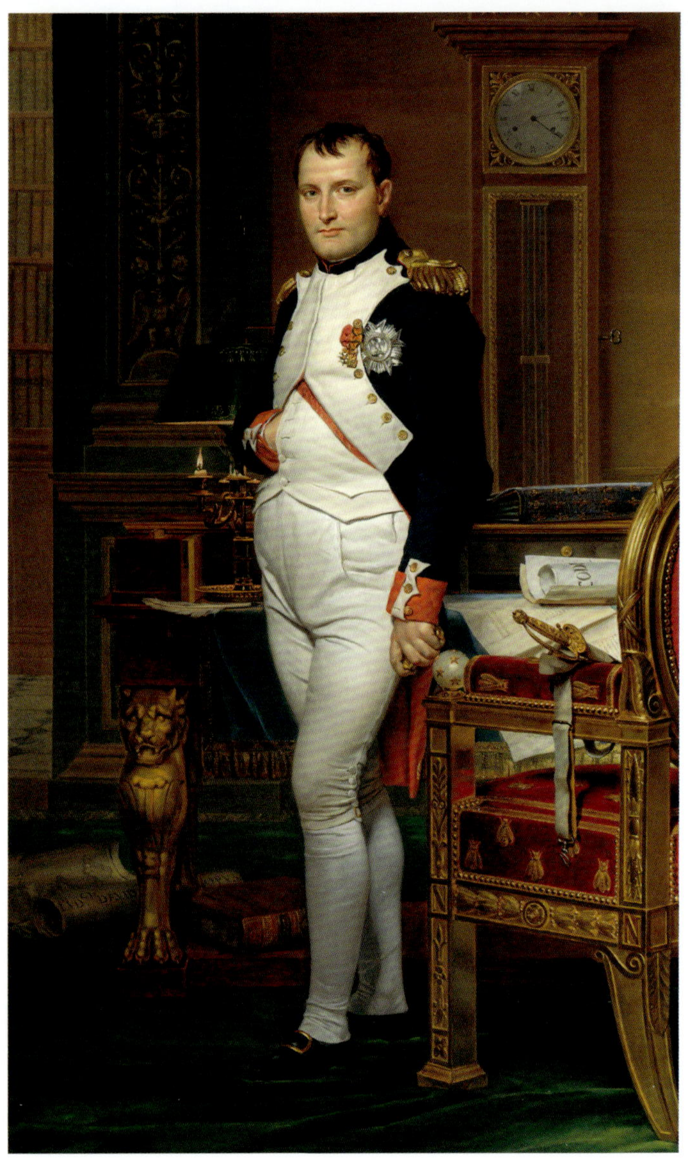

Jacques-Louis David
French, 1748–1825

The Emperor Napoleon in His Study at the Tuileries
1812

oil on canvas

SAMUEL H. KRESS COLLECTION
1961.9.15

In this full-length portrait of the French leader Napoleon Bonaparte, the emperor looks like he's had a late night. His stockings are wrinkled, his cuffs are unbuttoned, and his hair is disheveled. The painter Jacques-Louis David does not portray the powerful ruler on horseback in a moment of glory, as might be expected. David instead shows the emperor in his opulent study, where he is composing the Napoleonic Code, the foundation for much of French law today. Notice the quill on his desk, the heap of papers, the candles burned down to stubs, and the clock that reads 4:13 in the morning.

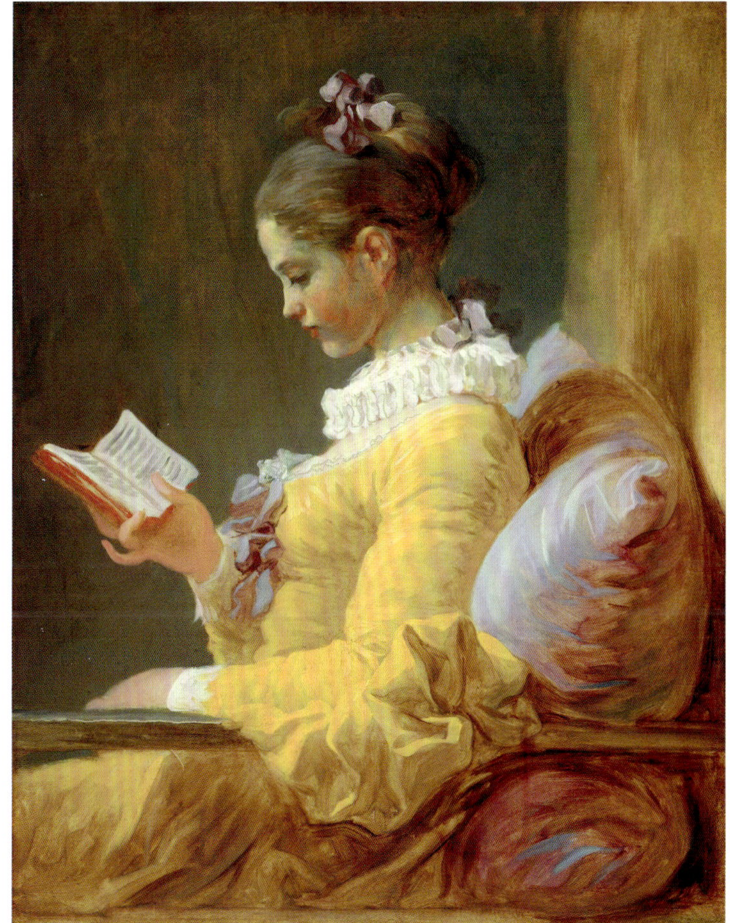

Jean Honoré Fragonard
French, 1732–1806

Young Girl Reading
c. 1769

oil on canvas

GIFT OF MRS. MELLON BRUCE IN MEMORY OF HER FATHER, ANDREW W. MELLON
1961.16.1

Light falls on the book a young woman holds in her hand. Absorbed in the story, she is unaware of our fixation on her profile. Her sumptuous lemon-colored dress, frilly ruff, and elegant bodice and ribbons are the brilliant results of Jean Honoré Fragonard's energetic brushwork, layered in shades of yellow and mauve. The artist used various techniques in painting this portrait. He created the lace of the ruff and bodice, for example, by dragging his brush handle through the paint while it was still wet.

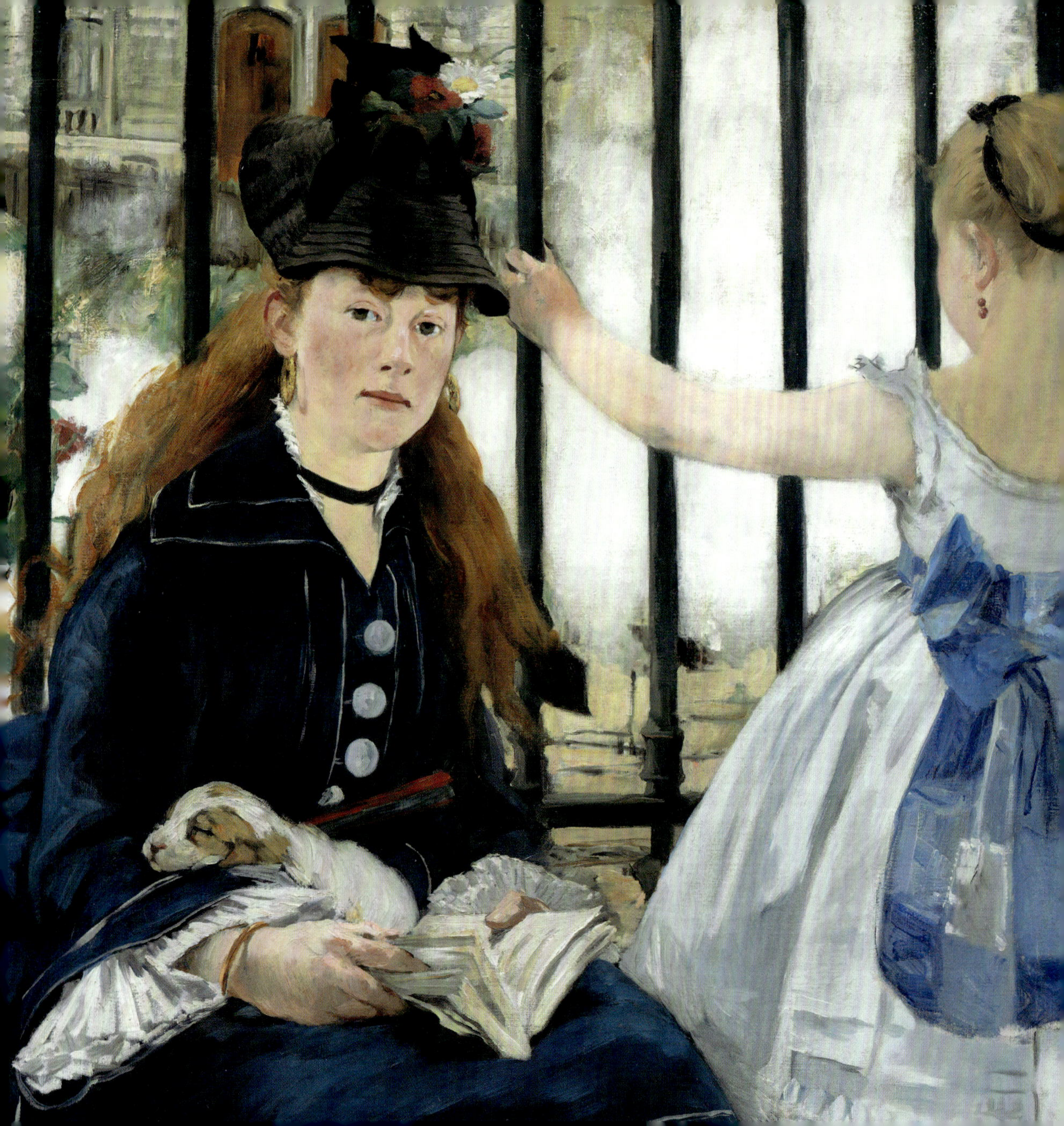

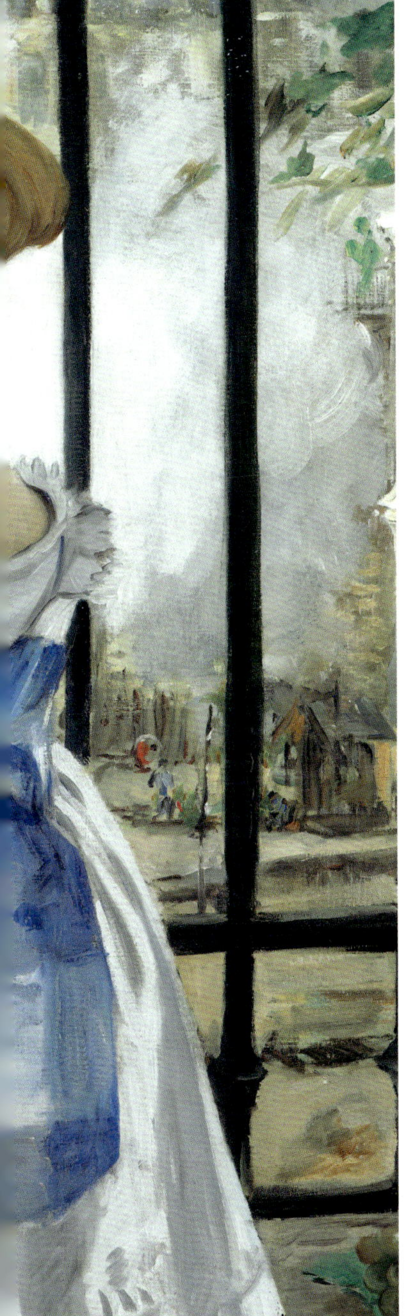

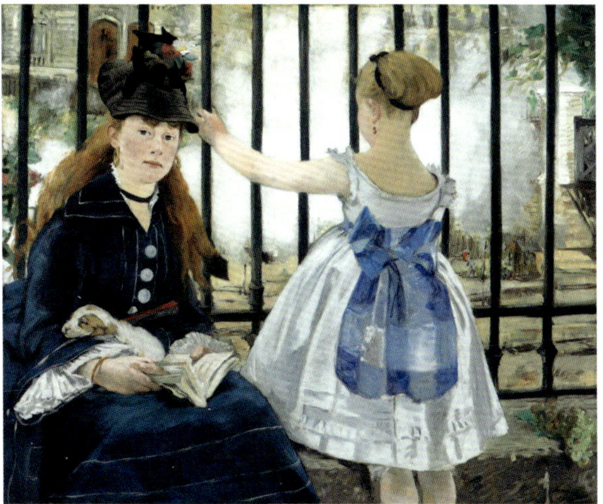

Edouard Manet
French, 1832–1883

The Railway
1873

oil on canvas

GIFT OF HORACE HAVEMEYER IN MEMORY
OF HIS MOTHER, LOUISINE W. HAVEMEYER
1956.10.1

Edouard Manet offers an intriguing study in contrasts and ambiguity in *The Railway*, starting with the relationship between the two figures. Are they mother and daughter? A nanny with a child? The girl gazes through the iron fence, where steam billows up from the tracks below. Wearing a white dress with an enormous blue bow, she is the visual opposite of the seated woman, who wears a blue ensemble with white trim topped by a fashionable black hat. The girl's locks are held up by a thin black ribbon, while the other figure's long hair is down. The child keeps her back to us; the woman looks us in the eye.

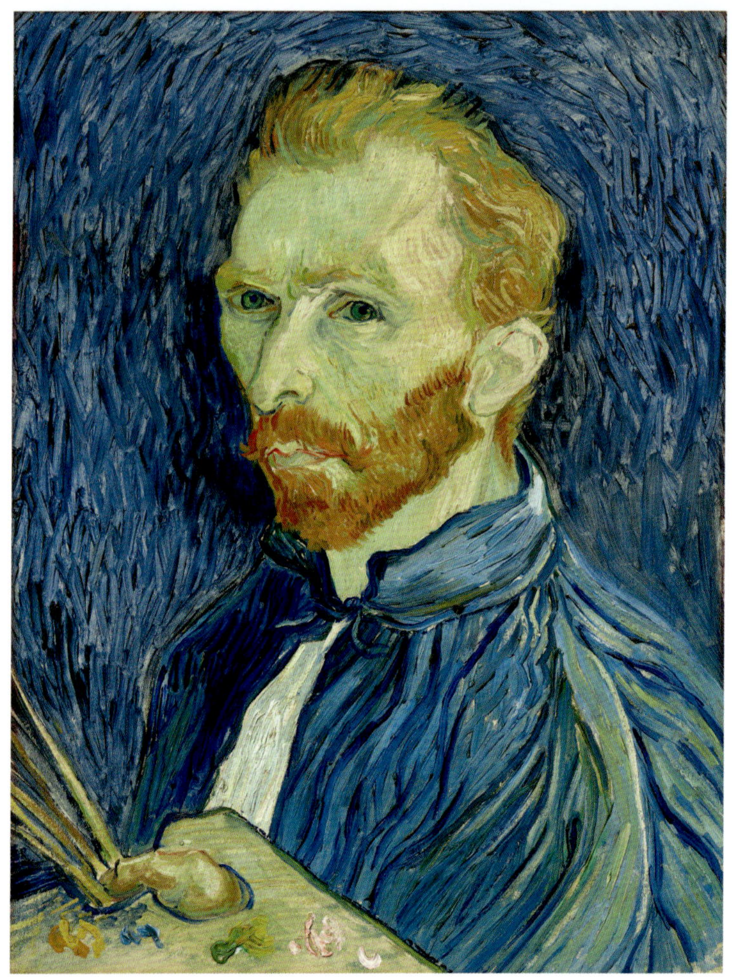

Vincent van Gogh
Dutch, 1853–1890

Self-Portrait
1889

oil on canvas

COLLECTION OF MR. AND MRS. JOHN HAY WHITNEY
1998.74.5

Vincent van Gogh painted 36 self-portraits. This was one of his last. Made at the asylum of Saint-Paul-de-Mausole in Saint-Rémy, where the artist was recovering from a severe breakdown, it is intense in every way. The swirling brushstrokes around his head are dynamic, the blues and violets of his smock are electric, and his narrowed gaze is unwavering. The artist's bright orange hair and rust-colored beard accentuate his sallow skin and add to his gaunt appearance. Still working despite his illness, Van Gogh keeps a tight grip on his brushes and palette.

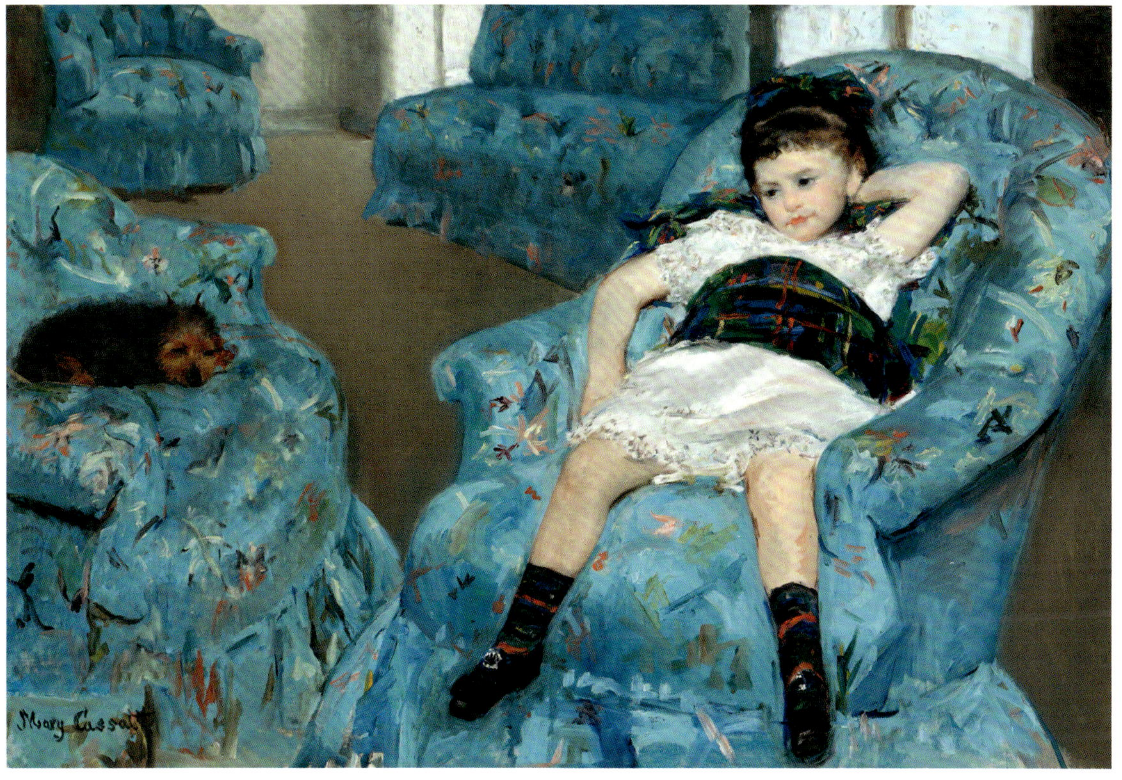

Mary Cassatt
American, 1844–1926

Little Girl in a Blue Armchair
1878

oil on canvas

COLLECTION OF MR. AND MRS. PAUL MELLON
1983.1.18

Boredom—or exhaustion—rarely looks as pleasurable as it does in this painting by impressionist artist Mary Cassatt. Before us are two overstuffed blue armchairs, one holding a small dog, the other a little girl. The child sinks into the poofy cushions. Bathed in light from the large windows, she supports her neck with a bent arm and stares into space. No one else is in the room, only more blue armchairs that serve as flowered attendants. Painted with free strokes of color, they form playful shapes and add depth to the scene.

Archibald John Motley Jr.
American, 1891–1981

Portrait of My Grandmother
1922

oil on canvas

PATRONS' PERMANENT FUND,
AVALON FUND, AND MOTLEY FUND
2018.2.1

When 80-year-old Emily Sims Motley posed for her grandson, her eyes focused on the artist working in front of her. That direct gaze now invites us to look carefully at this portrait. We take in the details of her lined yet regal face. Her white blouse is fastened with a heart-shaped pin. Her hands, worn and somewhat arthritic, rest gently in her aproned lap. Her slight shadow is behind her. After a while, we sense the love and respect that artist Archibald John Motley Jr. felt for this dignified elder, who was born enslaved and endured to live with four generations of her family in Chicago.

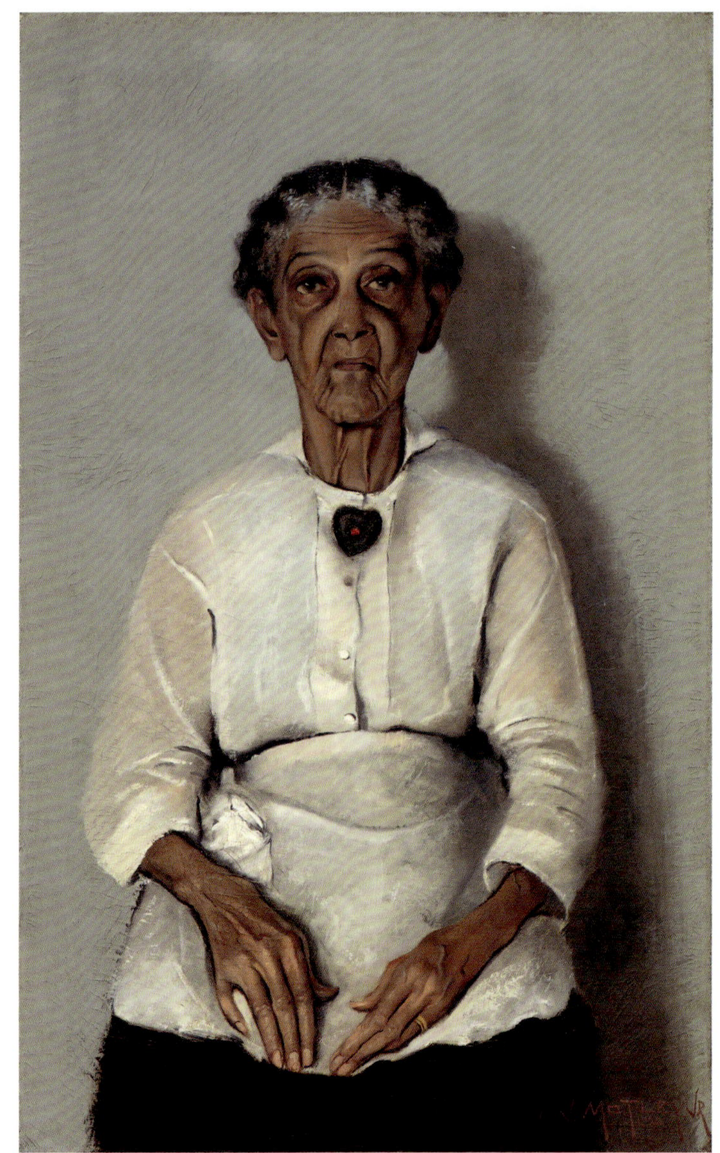

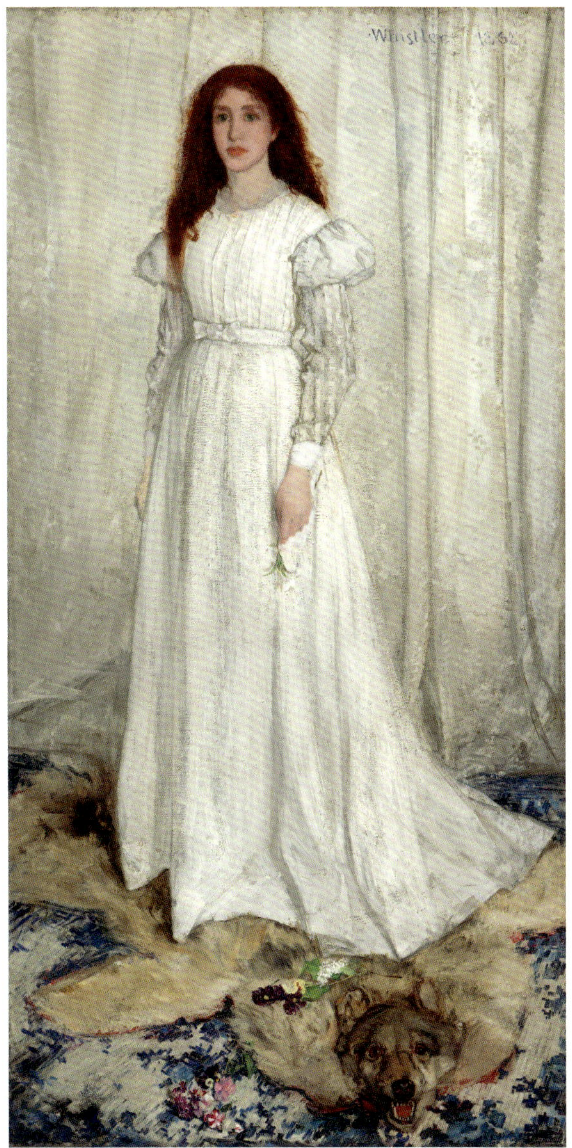

James McNeill Whistler
American, 1834–1903

Symphony in White, No. 1: The White Girl
1861–1863, 1872

oil on canvas

HARRIS WHITTEMORE COLLECTION
1943.6.2

An auburn-haired woman dressed entirely in white stands in front of a white curtain with a white flower in her hand. There is an elusive quality about her. The 1863 Paris Salon rejected this work, originally called *The White Girl*, because the style was too abstract for the times, and the subject—James McNeill Whistler's model and collaborator Joanna Hiffernan—was too suggestive. Whistler retitled the picture *Symphony in White*, a musical reference to his masterful application of white paint, which actually includes traces of yellow, red, blue, green, and black. Today this radical portrait is an icon of American art.

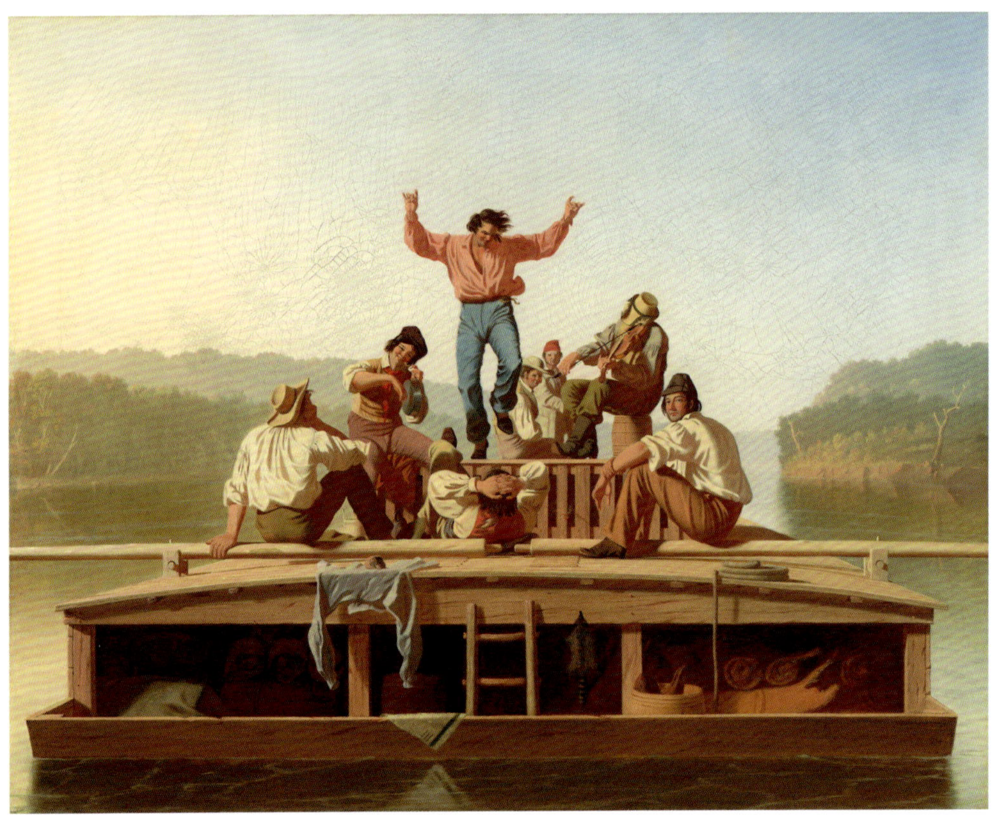

George Caleb Bingham
American, 1811–1879

The Jolly Flatboatmen
1846

oil on canvas

PATRONS' PERMANENT FUND
2015.18.1

Sunlight bathes the landscape and warms the men on the flat-bottomed boat. We float along with them as they relax after a day's work hauling cargo. A man at center dances joyfully to music provided by his companions. The others look on, except the man on the right, who turns toward us. George Caleb Bingham painted many works about life on and along the Missouri and Mississippi Rivers. His knowledge of the American West is evident in the abundance of detail—a raccoon pelt, coiled rope, a turkey peeking through a slatted crate, a blue shirt hanging to dry—in this idyllic scene.

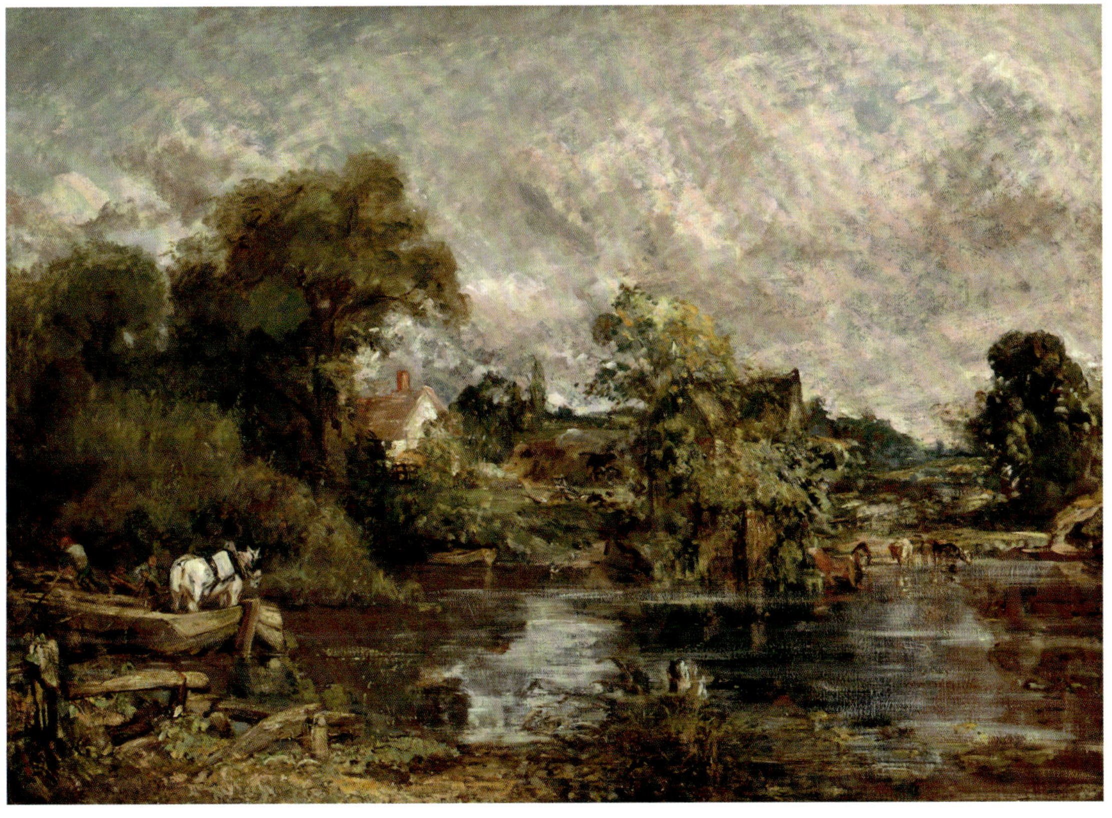

John Constable
British, 1776–1837

The White Horse
1818–1819

oil on canvas

WIDENER COLLECTION
1942.9.9

The white horse on the left occupies only a small part of this grand canvas. Harnessed and wearing blinders, it stands in a shallow barge, attended by two men. We can make out the English country cottage and other horses in the distance of the lush landscape, which is a confusing blur of loose brushstrokes. It seems the artist was in a hurry or left the work unfinished. In fact, researchers discovered that this work by John Constable is a sketch for a later canvas. They were also surprised to find evidence of an earlier painting under the charming scene we see today.

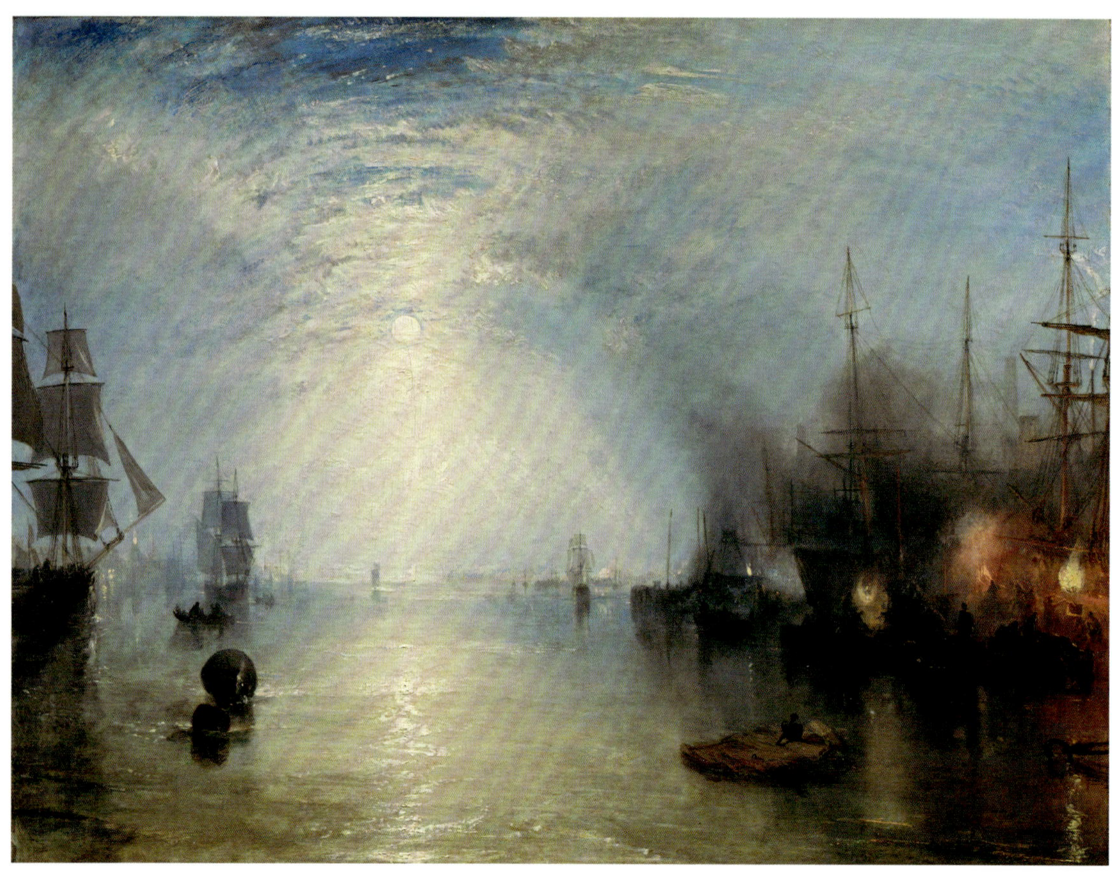

Joseph Mallord William Turner
British, 1775–1851

Keelmen Heaving in Coals by Moonlight
1835

oil on canvas

WIDENER COLLECTION
1942.9.86

Only a Romantic painter of J.M.W. Turner's genius could turn coal into poetry. In this radiant canvas he softens the gritty labor of transferring coal to sailing ships by distracting us with a dazzling moon. Like a beacon, it creates a sparkling path from the horizon through the center of the channel. On the left, ships with hoisted sails are ready to depart. On the right, flat-bottomed keels supply coal to waiting vessels. The warm colors of the keelmen's fiery torches provide a visual balance to the swirling blue sky.

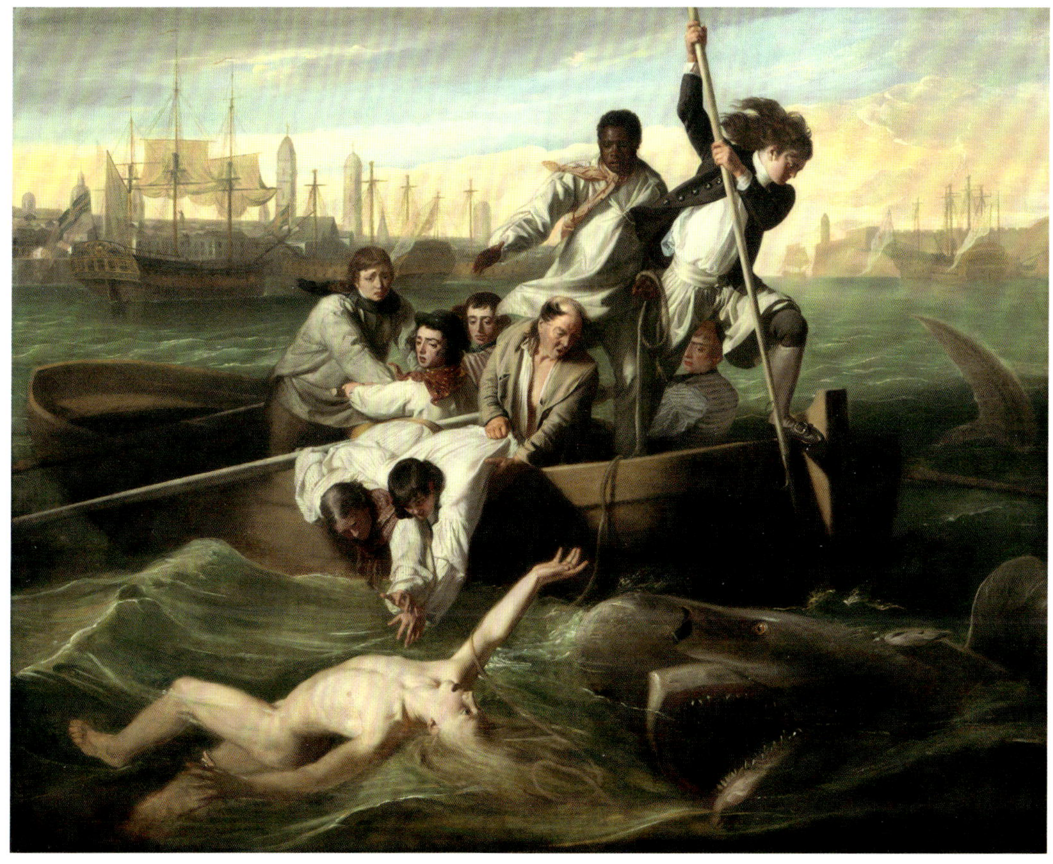

John Singleton Copley
American, 1738–1815

Watson and the Shark
1778

oil on canvas

FERDINAND LAMMOT BELIN FUND
1963.6.1

This painting is based on a true account of a shark attack in Havana Harbor in 1749. John Singleton Copley depicts a critical moment in the attempted rescue of 14-year-old Brook Watson. The young swimmer has already lost a foot to the shark. Will he lose his life as the shark circles back for another attack? Horror and panic grip many of the nine rescuers in the boat. Only the Black sailor at center appears in control as he holds a life-saving rope that links him to the boy. His prominence is particularly significant: Cuba was a major port in the transatlantic slave trade.

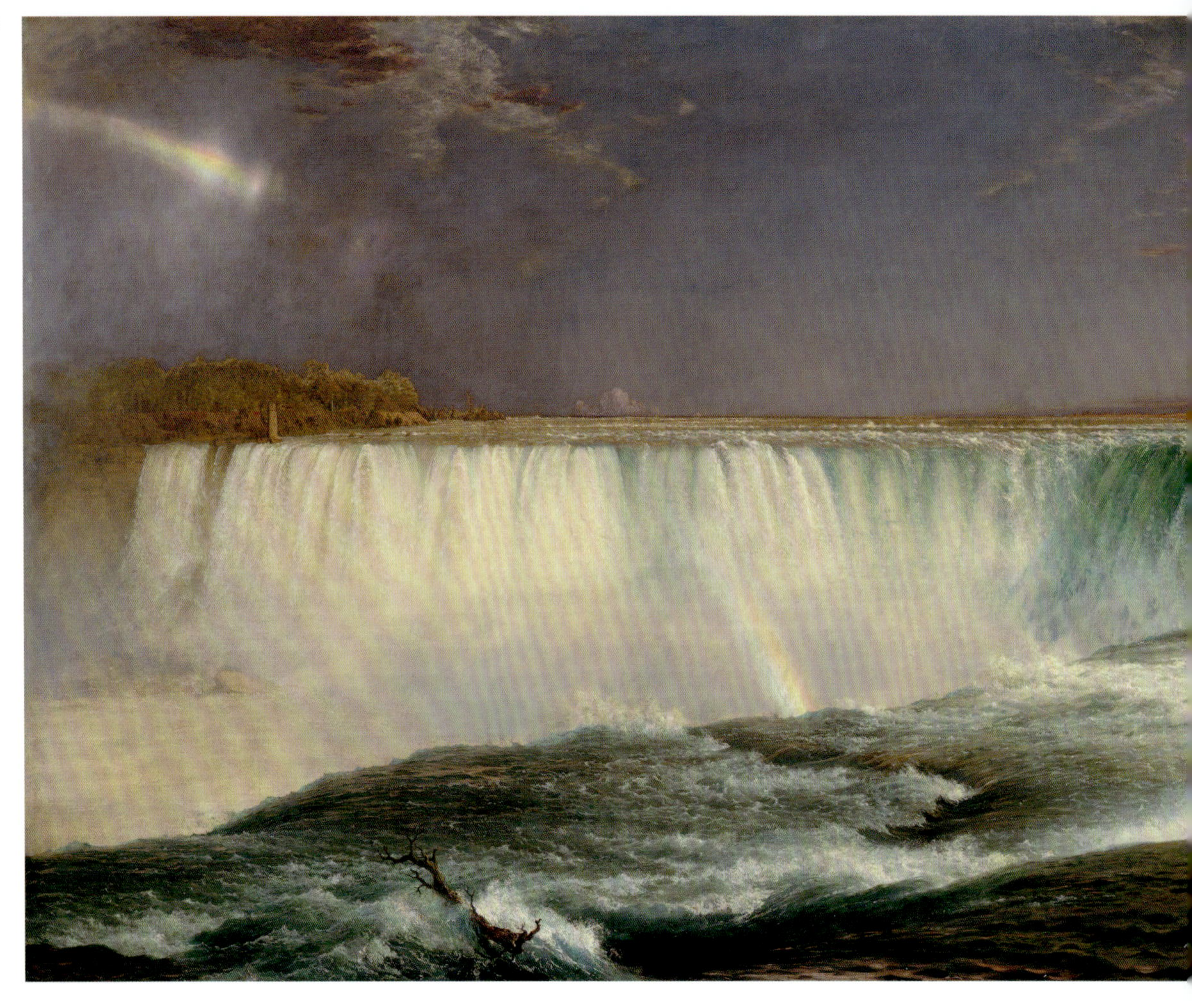

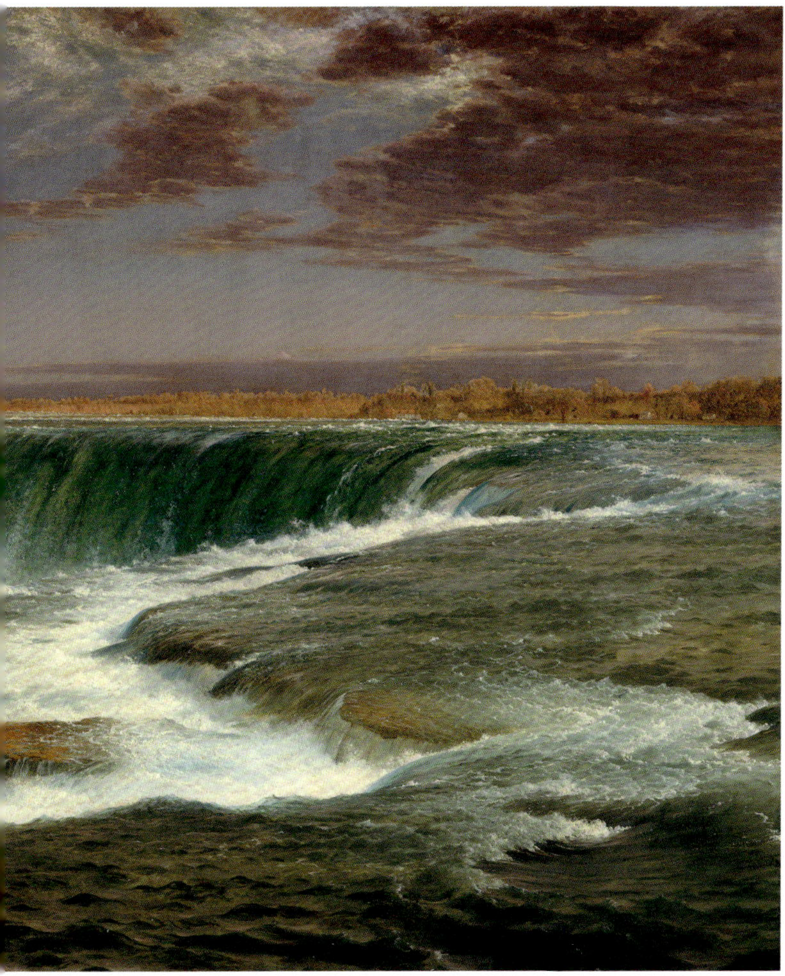

Frederic Edwin Church
American, 1826–1900

Niagara
1857

oil on canvas

CORCORAN COLLECTION (MUSEUM PURCHASE, GALLERY FUND, 1876)
2014.79.10

If this monumental canvas came with sound, it would be a deafening roar. Frederic Edwin Church's great panorama places us at eye level with this natural wonder. It seems we could reach into the churning green rapids and feel the rush of falling, swirling, and spraying water. Such marvelous illusion drew thousands of people to see this painting of Niagara Falls when it toured the country after Church completed it in 1857. The work sealed Church's reputation as the most famous American painter of his time.

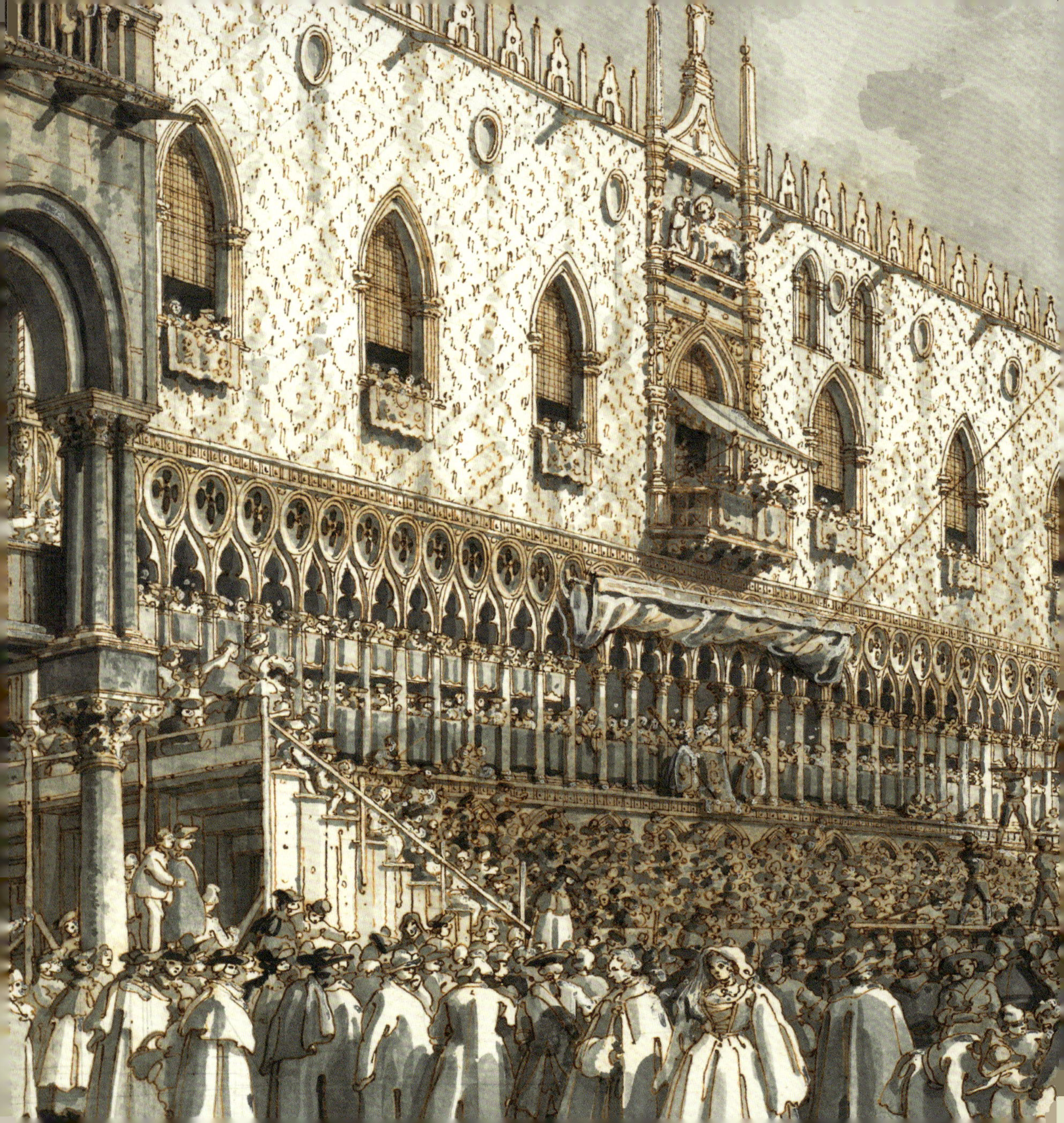

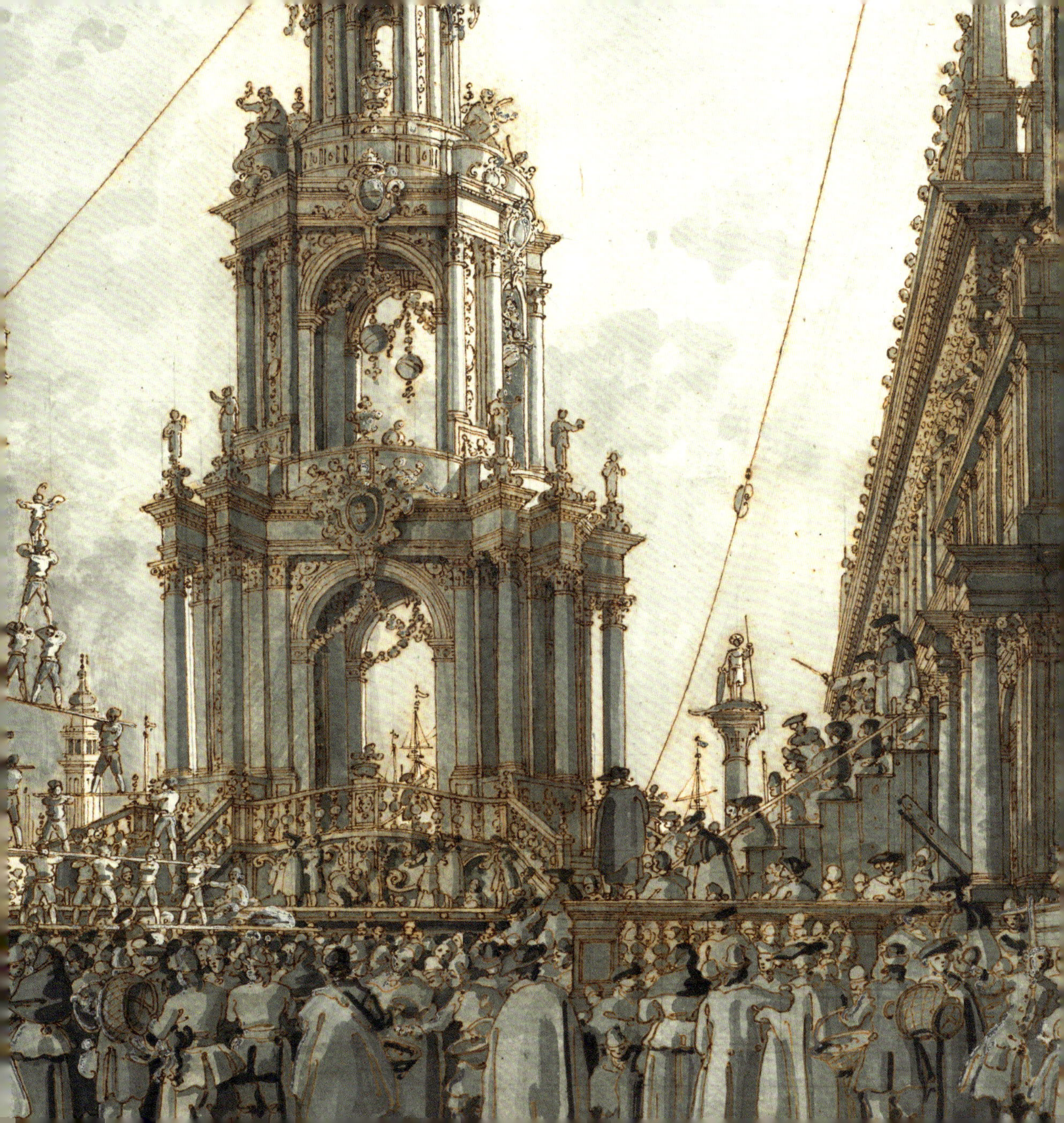

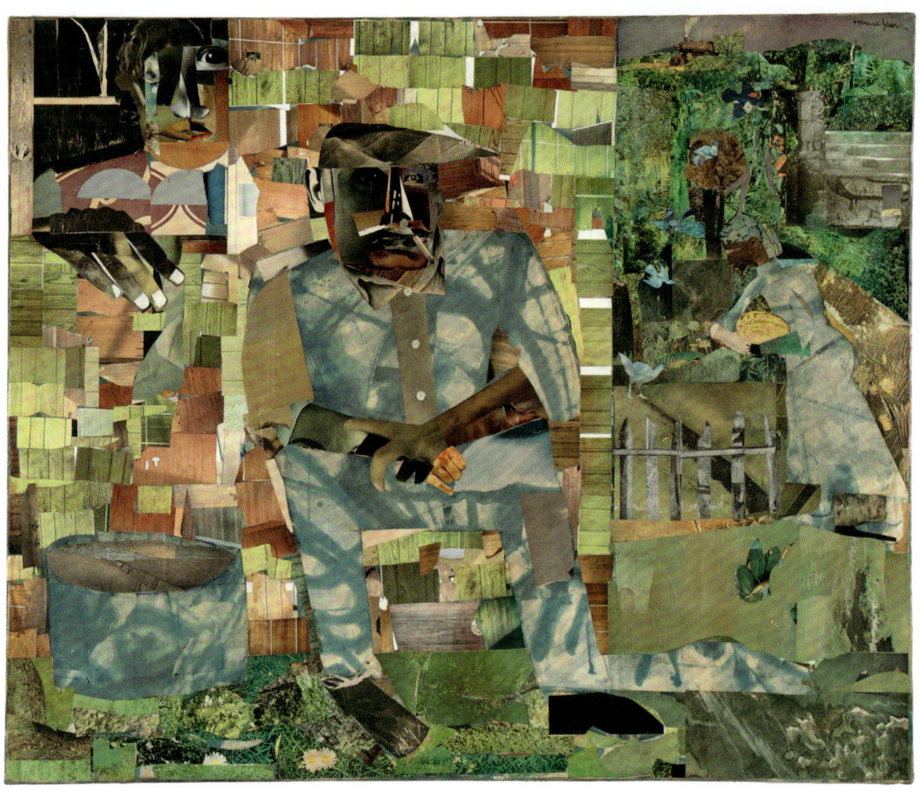

Romare Bearden
American, 1911–1988

Tomorrow I May Be Far Away
1967

collage of various papers with charcoal, graphite, and paint on paper mounted to canvas

PAUL MELLON FUND
2001.72.1

Much like Edith Johnson's 1929 classic song "Good Chib Blues," Romare Bearden's intricate collage tells a story through repetition and rhythm. Here, clippings in shades of green, blue, tan, and brown create a powerful composition based on the artist's childhood memories of rural North Carolina. A large man seated in the center leans against a structure reminiscent of a sharecropper's cabin. One woman peers out from the window nearby while another tends to chickens in the yard. The title, based on the song's lyrics, suggests Bearden's bittersweet ties to the South: "Aah, tomorrow I may be far away/Oh, tomorrow I may be far away/Don't try to jive me, sweet talk can't make me stay."

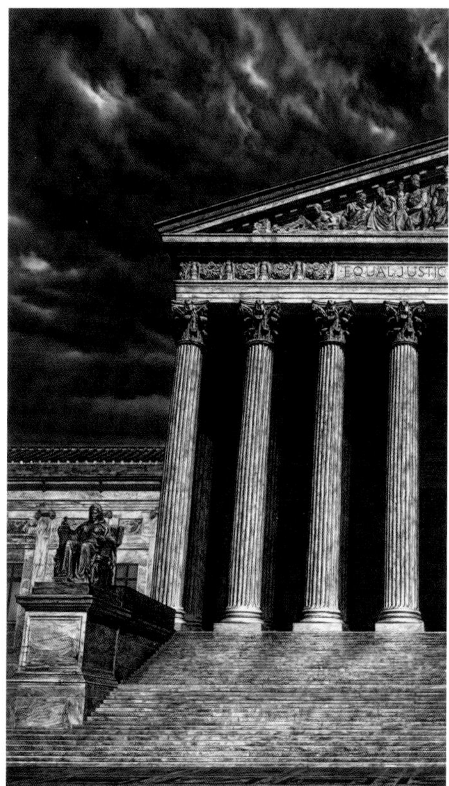

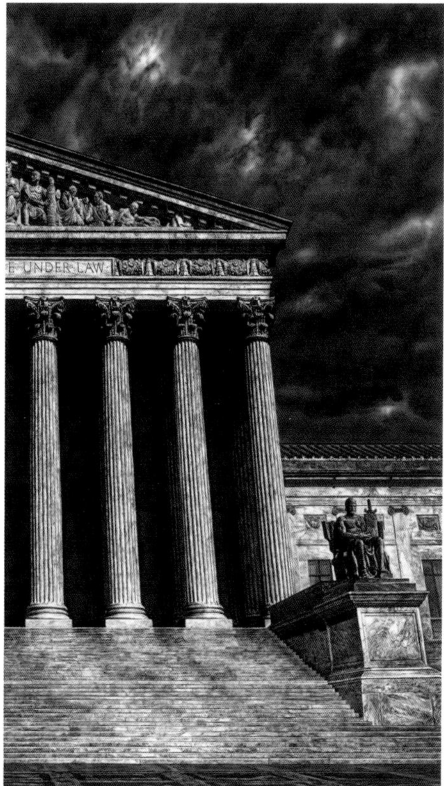

Robert Longo
American, born 1953

The Rock (The Supreme Court of the United States—Split)

2018

charcoal on paper mounted to aluminum panels

GIFT OF CLIFFORD ROSS
2023.6.3.A-B

The enormous size of this work is astounding—and confounding. Is it a colossal photograph? Astonishingly, it is a highly realistic and meticulously detailed charcoal drawing. The work itself is as monumental as its subject, the US Supreme Court building in Washington, DC. Why did the artist split the magnificent façade of the building in two? When Robert Longo made this drawing in 2018, there were four liberal and four conservative justices on the Supreme Court. The separate panels refer to that division. The dark clouds gathering above the highest judicial body in the United States hint at its stormy future.

Winslow Homer
American, 1836–1910

Blackboard
1877

watercolor on wove paper

GIFT OF JO ANN AND JULIAN GANZ, JR., IN HONOR OF THE 50TH ANNIVERSARY OF THE NATIONAL GALLERY OF ART
1990.60.1

Drawing, an important component of industrial design, was a required subject taught in Massachusetts public schools in the 1870s. Looking not much older than the students who presumably sit at their desks behind her, a young teacher leads a class on the basic principles of drawing. Geometric shapes—triangles, circles, squares, rectangles—fill the blackboard. Winslow Homer ingeniously puts these forms into practice in this watercolor. Follow the triangle formed from the bow at the top of her head down to her bent elbow, across her back, and up her right side. Homer adds himself in the lesson by signing his name on the blackboard.

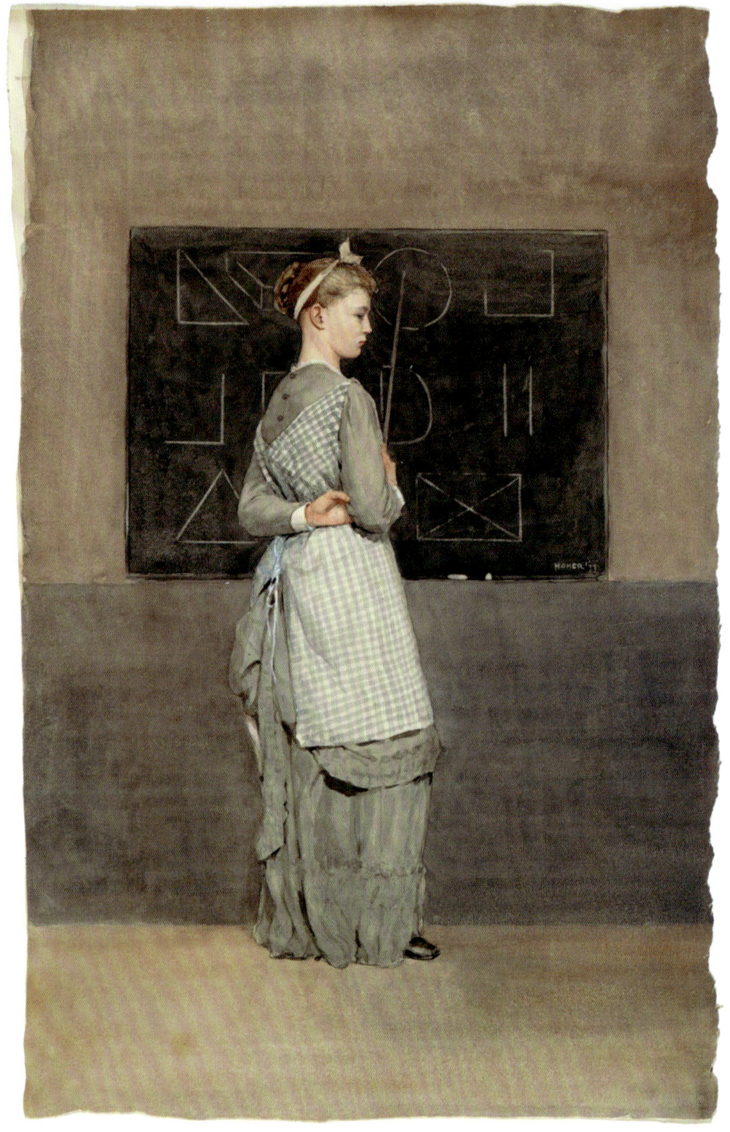

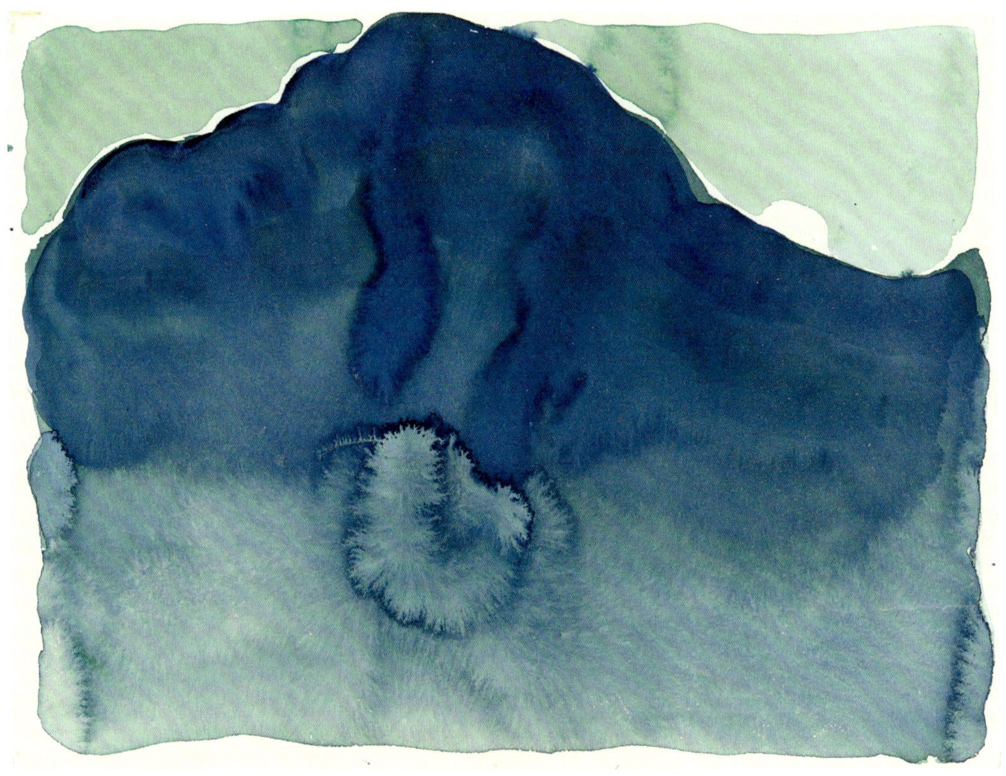

Georgia O'Keeffe
American, 1887–1986

Blue Hill No. 1
1916

watercolor on wove paper

GIFT OF JOAN AND LUCIO NOTO AND THE GEORGIA O'KEEFFE FOUNDATION
2002.11.1

She was bold and different—and so was her art. The soft and subtle *Blue Hill No. 1,* an early example of Georgia O'Keeffe's distinctive "voice," marks a turning point in the career of this esteemed modern artist. Inspired by the hills of the Blue Ridge Mountains near the University of Virginia, where she taught in 1916, O'Keeffe moved away from representing or copying what she saw to conveying the feeling she experienced. She simplified forms, and her works became more abstract, as seen in this watercolor. Later, she applied her unique vision to paintings of flowers, New York City skyscrapers, and New Mexico landscapes.

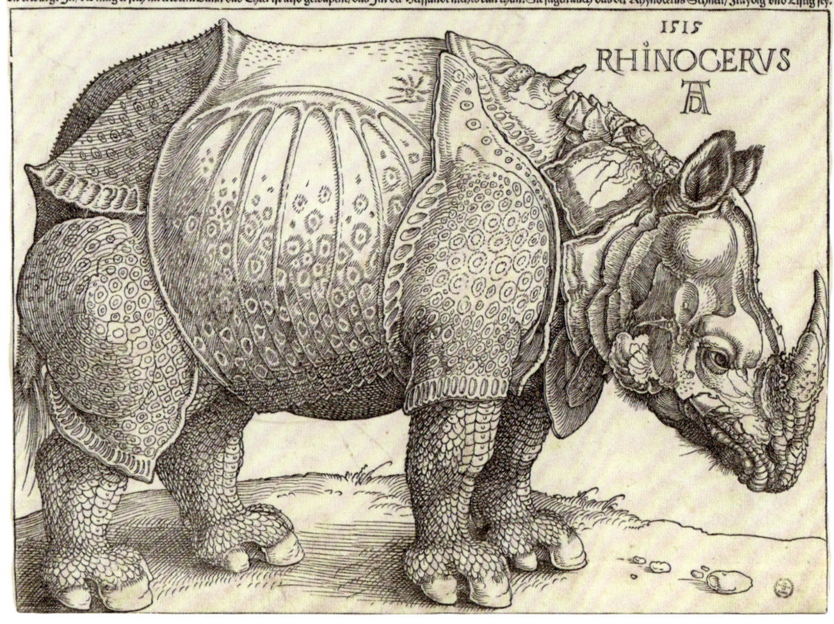

Albrecht Dürer
German, 1471–1528

The Rhinoceros
1515

woodcut on laid paper

ROSENWALD COLLECTION
1964.8.697

The text at the top of this print states in German: "On 1 May 1513 was brought from India to the great and powerful king Emanuel of Portugal to Lisbon such a live animal called a rhinoceros." As we can now tell from this intricately carved woodcut, the artist Albrecht Dürer never actually saw the animal. For one thing, his rhinoceros wears an amusing suit of chain mail and armor, like a medieval knight. The animal also has reptilian-like scales on its legs. Despite these inaccuracies, Dürer's woodcut was accepted as the standard image of a rhinoceros until the 18th century.

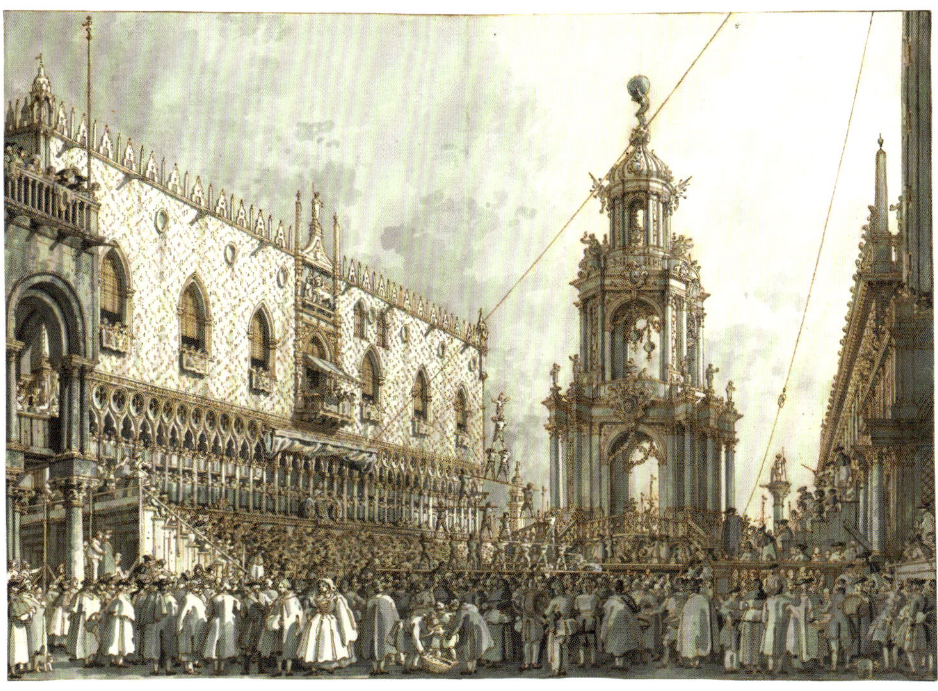

Canaletto
Venetian, 1697–1768

The "Giovedì Grasso" Festival before the Ducal Palace in Venice
1765/1766

pen and brown ink with gray wash over traces of graphite, tip of the brush with black wash, heightened with touches of white gouache (laid on thick 18th-century mount)

WOLFGANG RATJEN COLLECTION, PAUL MELLON FUND
2007.111.55

The Italian city of Venice is often crowded, but the throng in this drawing of the Ducal Palace on the festival of Giovedì Grasso (Fat Thursday) is unusually dense. Revelers pack the piazza and enjoy performances before the start of the Christian holy days of Lent. Daring acrobats balancing on thin poles seem to soar almost to the arched windows of the ornate palace. The masts of ships docked in the bustling port rise in the distance. Such splendid details, which capture the essence of his birthplace, earned Canaletto wide acclaim.

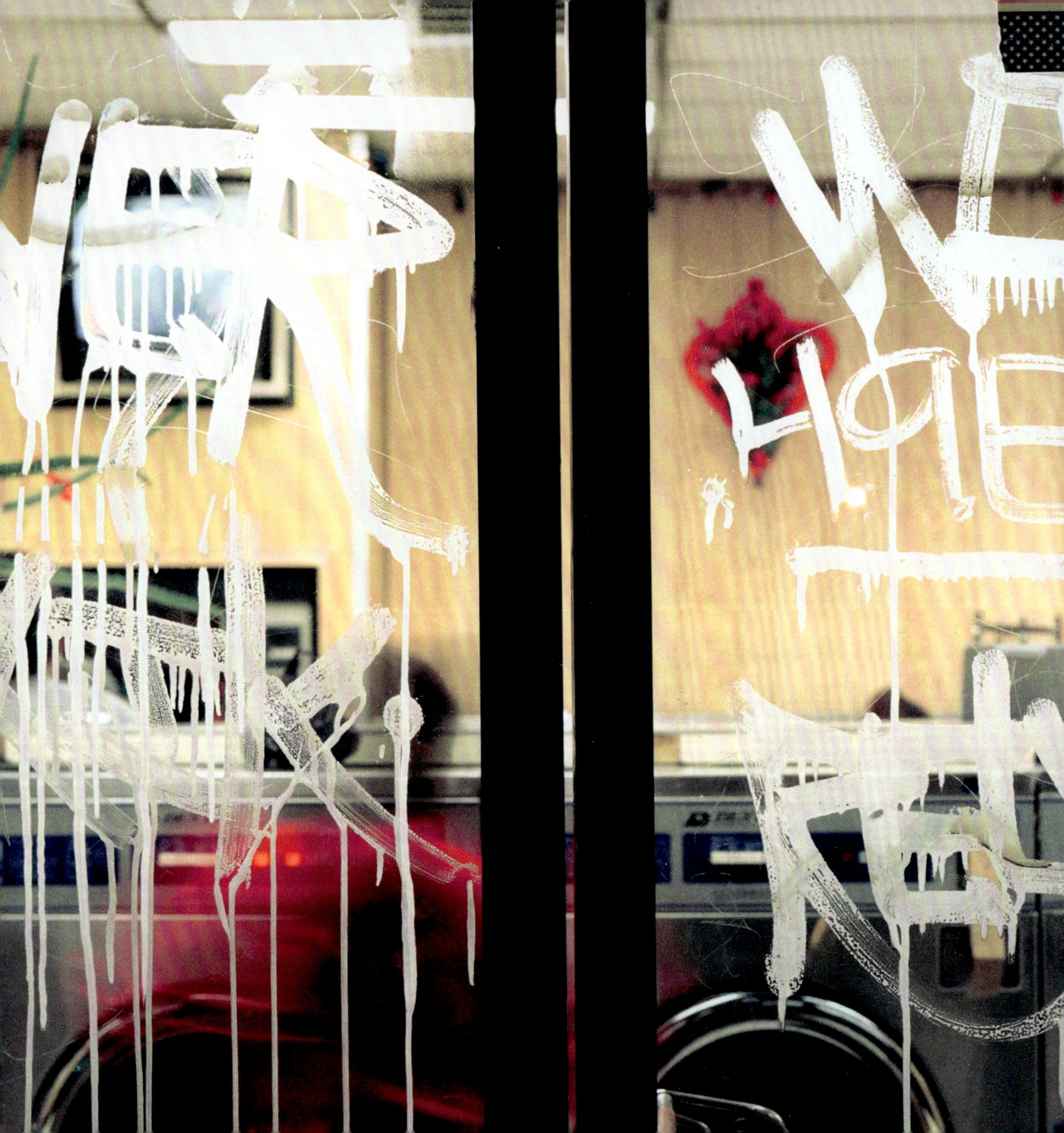

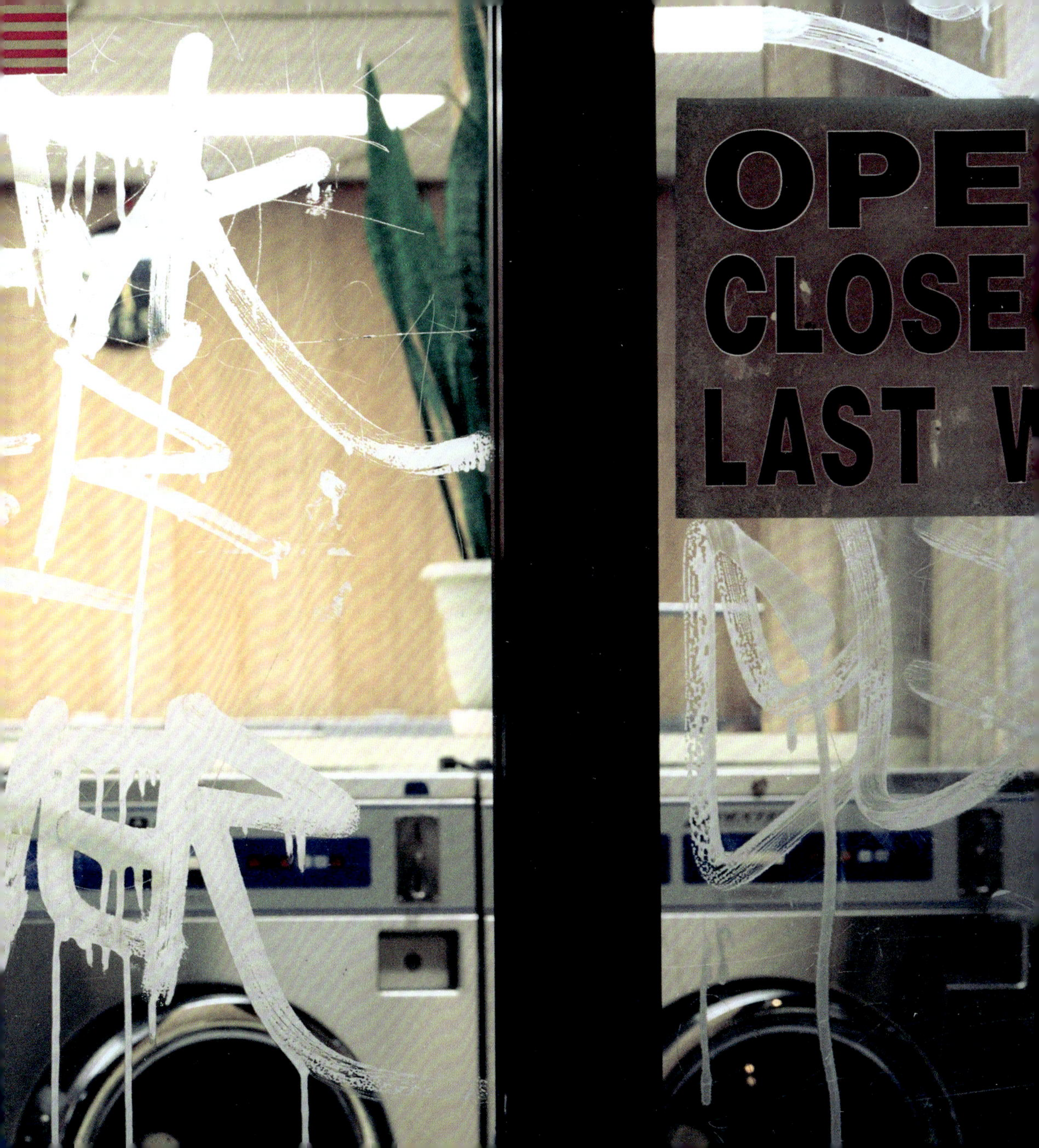

OPE
CLOSE
LAST W

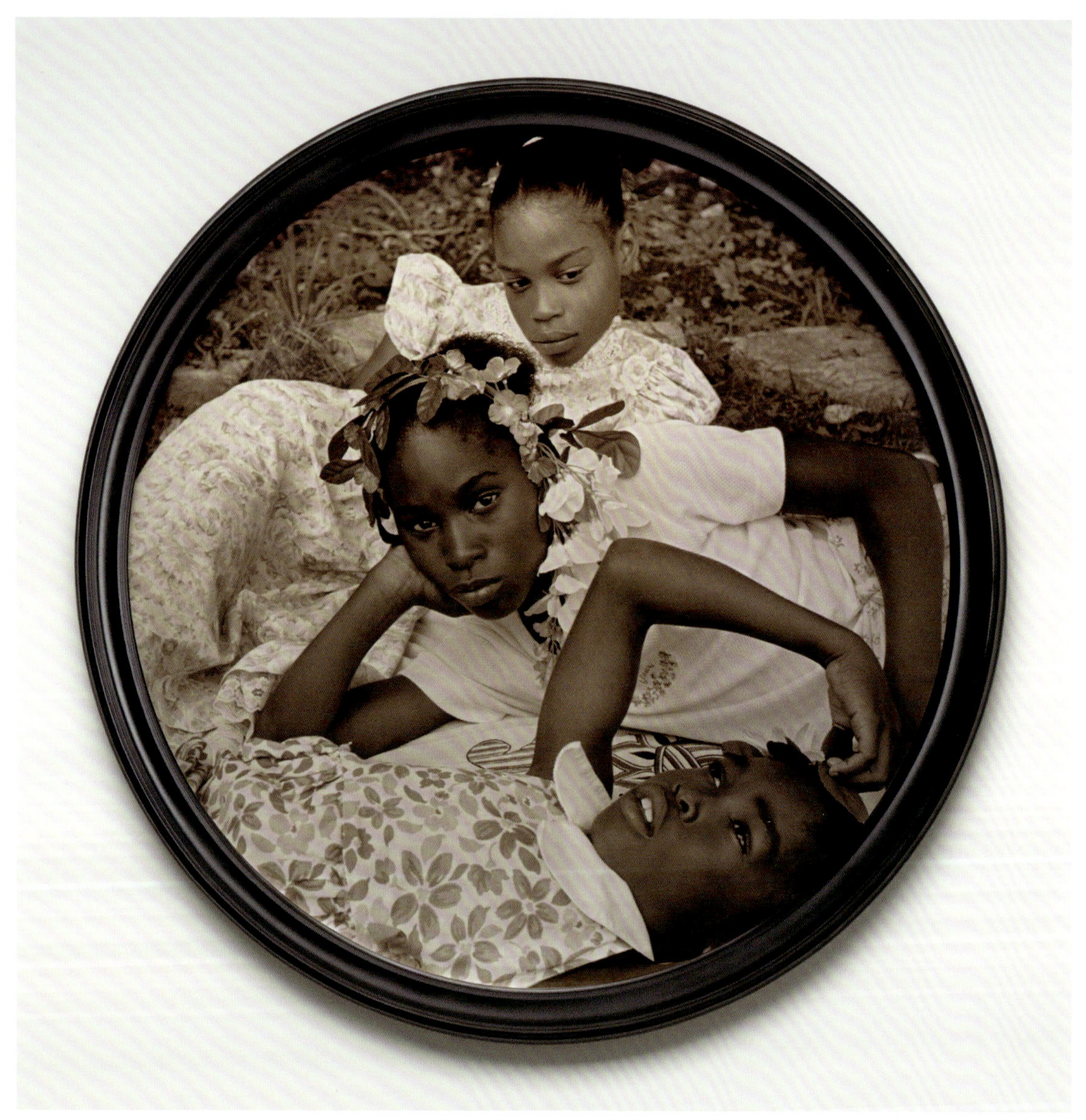

Carrie Mae Weems
American, born 1953

May Flowers
2002, printed 2013

chromogenic print

ALFRED H. MOSES AND FERN M. SCHAD FUND
2014.3.1

Photographs by Carrie Mae Weems make us look and think twice. At first glance, this seems to be a 19th-century sepia-toned print of three girls in an idyllic pastoral setting. They are tightly arranged within a circular frame, reminiscent of celestial angels in religious paintings from the Renaissance. When we look closer, we notice the expressions of these girls in floral dresses are focused and deliberate. The figure at center sizes us up, as if to dare us to include them in traditional art historical representations.

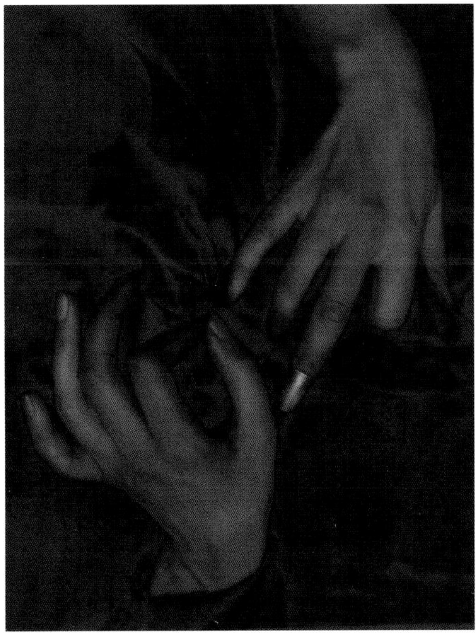

Alfred Stieglitz
American, 1864–1946

Georgia O'Keeffe—Hands and Thimble
1919

palladium print

ALFRED STIEGLITZ COLLECTION
1980.70.138

Is a picture a portrait if it doesn't include a face? Alfred Stieglitz took hundreds of photographs of his wife, artist Georgia O'Keeffe. Many focused on only a part of her body. He felt these images captured her essence. Here, her hands dance gracefully over dark swirling fabric. She clasps a sewing needle between the finger and thumb of one hand. A thimble caps a finger on the other. O'Keeffe was not only a pioneering painter but also an expert seamstress. Stieglitz's innovative approach to composing, cropping, and printing photographs made him an influential figure in 20th-century art.

Gordon Parks
American, 1912–2006

Self-Portrait
1941

gelatin silver print

PURCHASED AS THE GIFT OF ALAN AND MARSHA PALLER, LAURA ARRILLAGA-ANDREESSEN AND MARC ANDREESSEN VIA THE SILICON VALLEY COMMUNITY FOUNDATION, RAJ AND INDRA NOOYI, MITCHELL P. RALES, DAVID M. RUBENSTEIN, AND DARREN WALKER IN HONOR OF SHARON PERCY ROCKEFELLER
2021.61.1

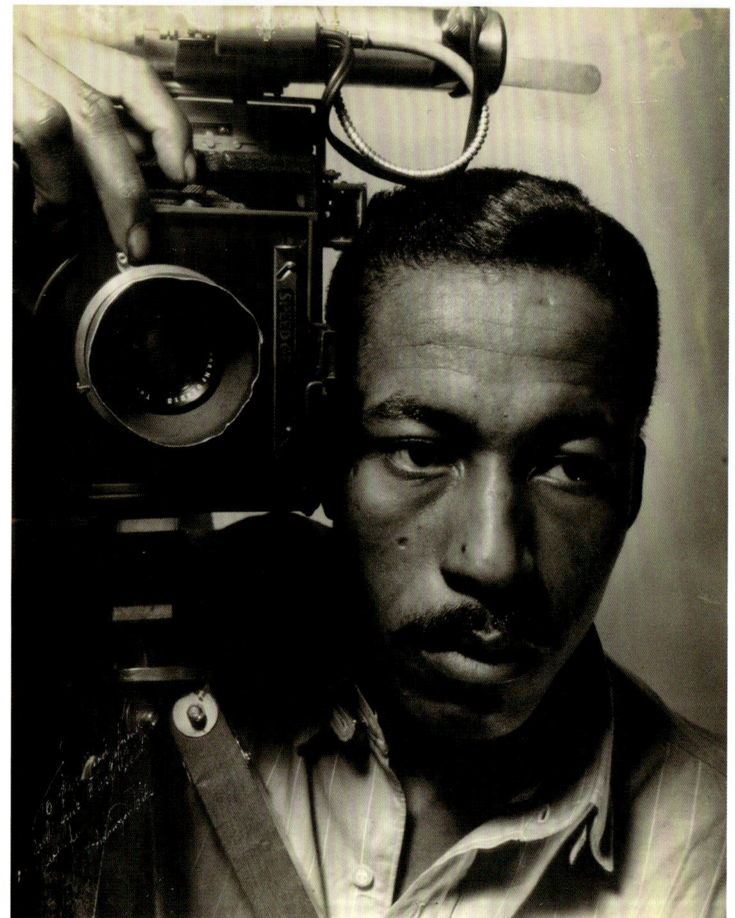

Gordon Parks wants us to know he's a photographer. He was 28 years old and just starting his career when he made this self-portrait. Look at the way he holds his camera level with his head, as if it's part of his identity. Parks used photographs, and later film, to fight against the racism he experienced all his life. Despite the obstacles he encountered, this self-taught artist became a successful photographer, contributing images to *Life*, *Vogue*, and *Ebony* magazines.

James Van Der Zee
American, 1886–1983

Portrait of a Couple
1924

gelatin silver print

ROBERT B. MENSCHEL FUND
2000.83.1

We don't know their names, but they are a lovely couple. He is dignified, with watch chain, derby, and cane. She is fashionable, in an embroidered dress adorned with modest jewelry, her hair styled in a 1920s bob. Although this is a formal studio portrait, a relaxed warmth fills the picture. Perhaps that is because James Van Der Zee was one of the most skilled photographers in New York's Harlem from the 1920s to the 1940s. He knew his clients and literally showed them in the best light. His photographs chronicle a vibrant community with a strong sense of identity.

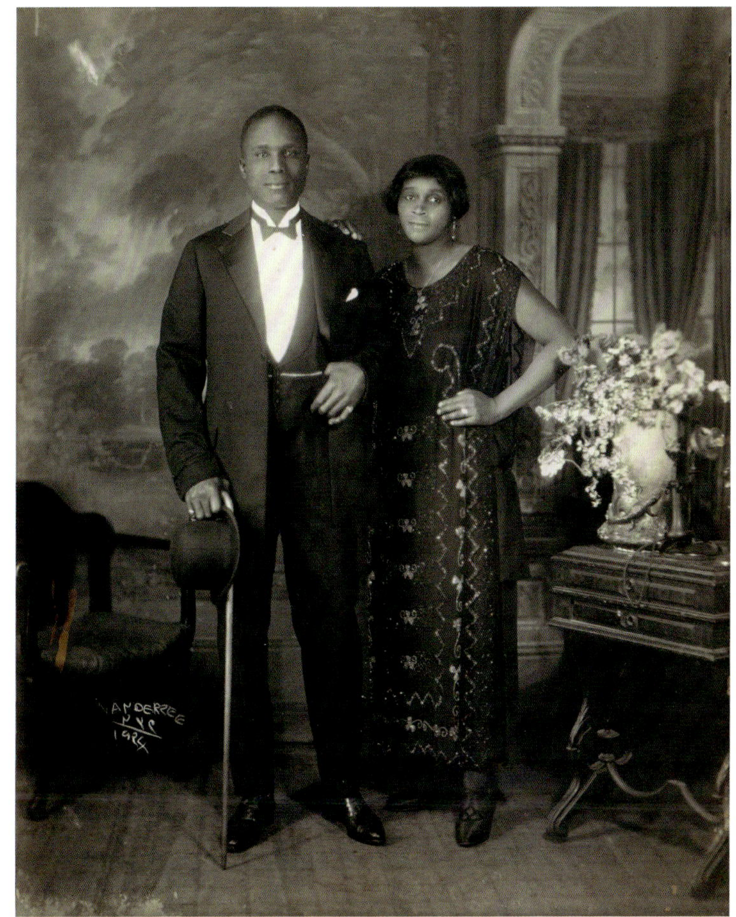

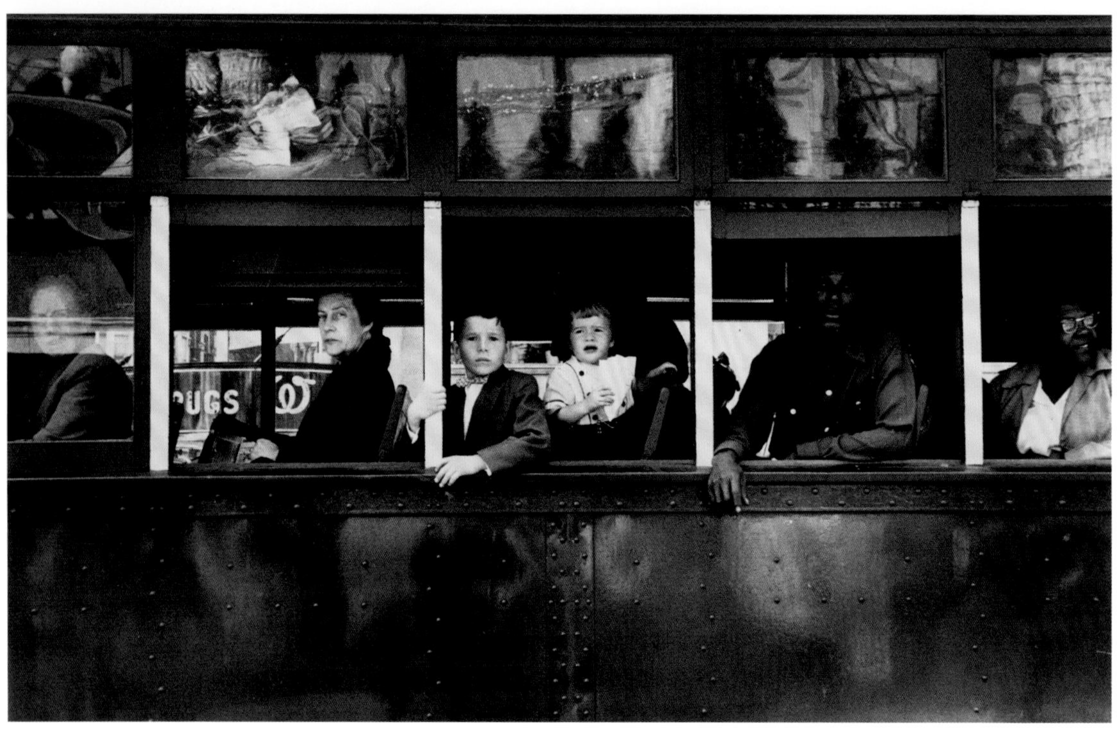

Robert Frank
American, born Switzerland, 1924–2019

Trolley—New Orleans
1955

gelatin silver print

GIFT OF MARIA AND LEE FRIEDLANDER
2001.8.1

Are there no happy riders on this New Orleans trolley? Each person stares from their own window as if jailed in their seat. With severe-looking white passengers in front and weary Black riders relegated to the back, the streetcar epitomizes segregated life in the American South in the 1950s. Photographer Robert Frank, a Swiss émigré to the United States, journeyed across the country in 1955 and 1956 to document American life. Through innovative photographs like this one, he revealed a society that, similar to the diverse gazes of the people on this trolley, was divided.

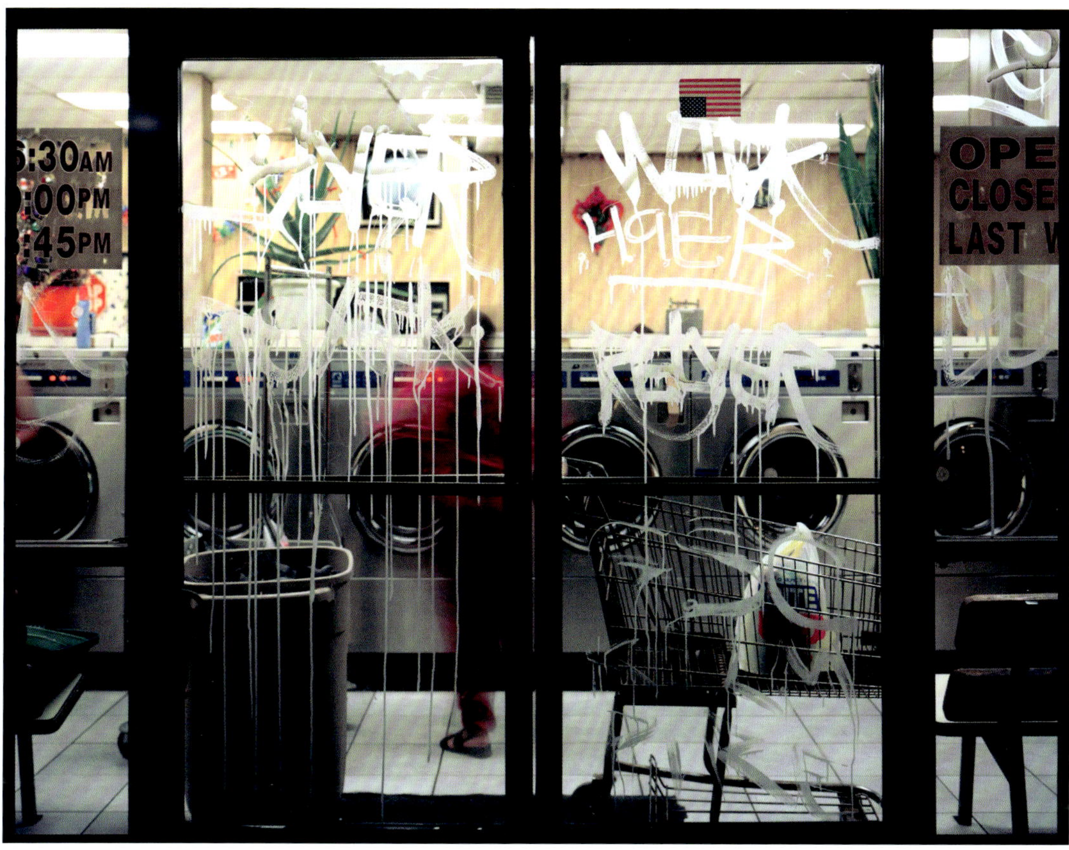

Christina Fernandez
American, born 1965

Lavanderia #1
2002, printed 2021

inkjet print

GIFT OF DAVID KNAUS
2022.46.1

On a dark night Christina Fernandez focused her camera lens on a brightly lit laundromat in the Boyle Heights neighborhood of Los Angeles. Through the graffiti-splattered doors we glimpse a blurred figure washing clothes. Many of the Mexican American residents who lived nearby had to tackle this domestic chore after a hard day of work. Inside, the metal machines are silent witnesses to the monotonous labor taking place. From the outside, we might be fascinated by the dripping graffiti or empathize with the unknown person performing this lonely task.

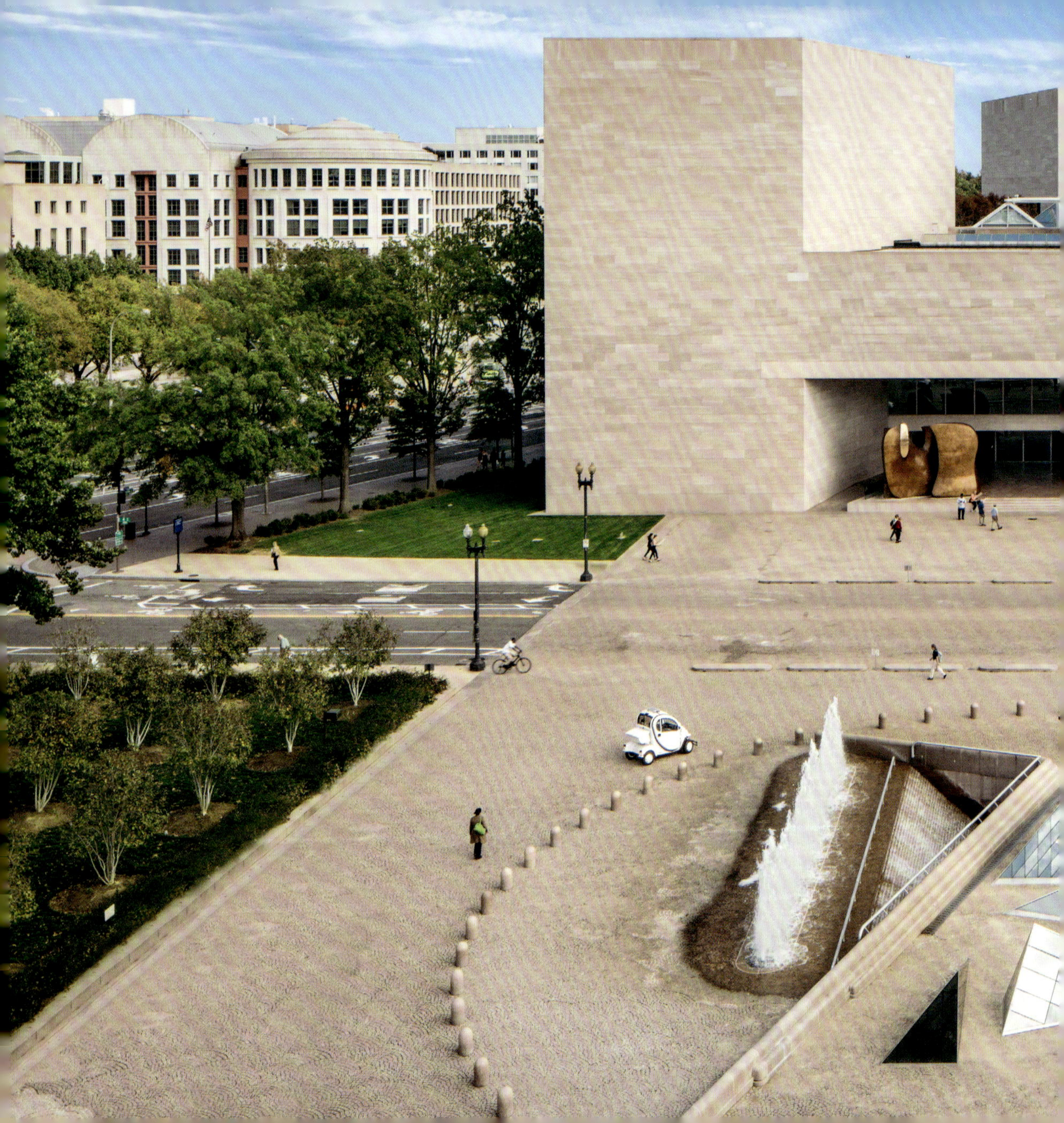

East Building

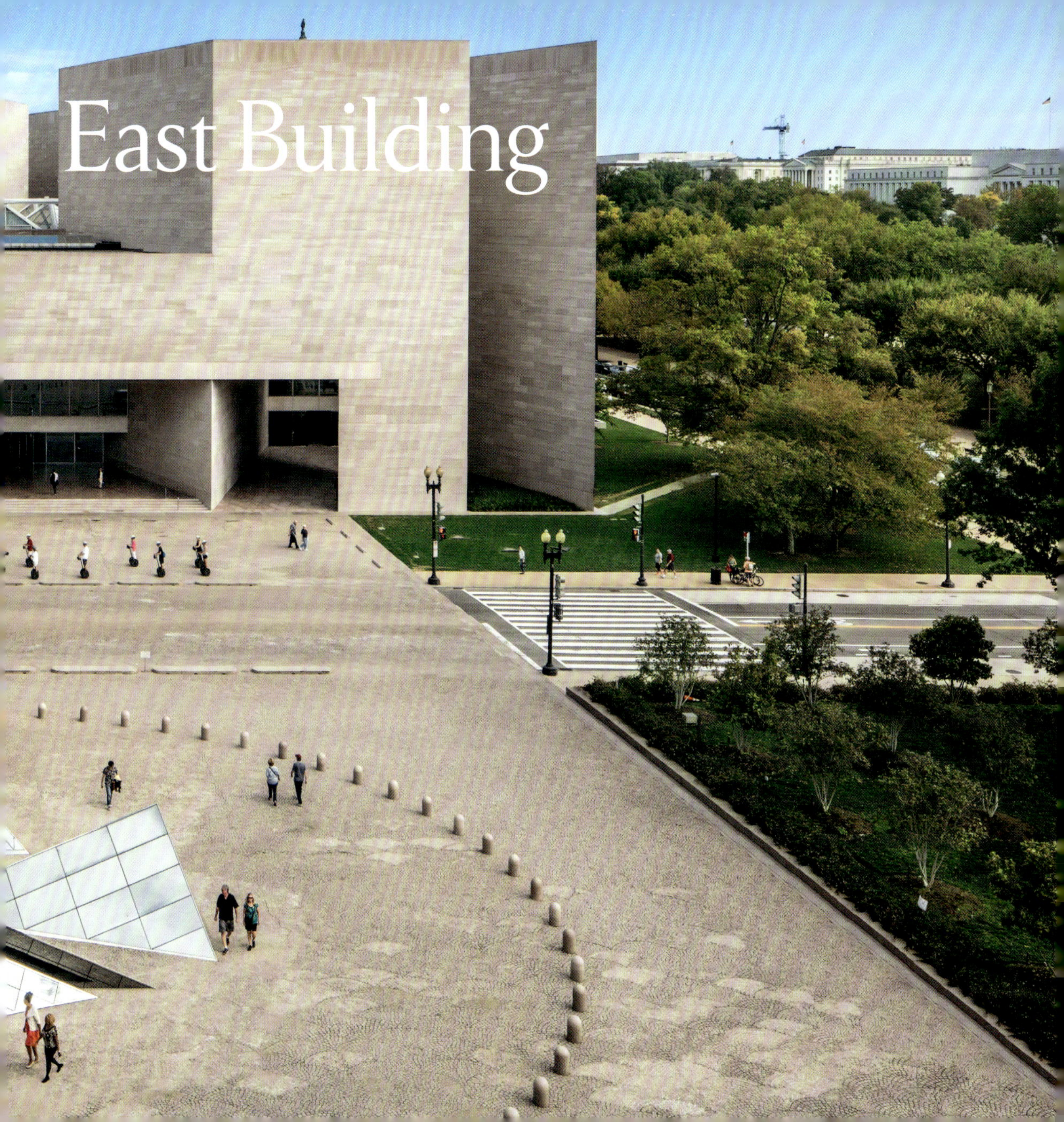

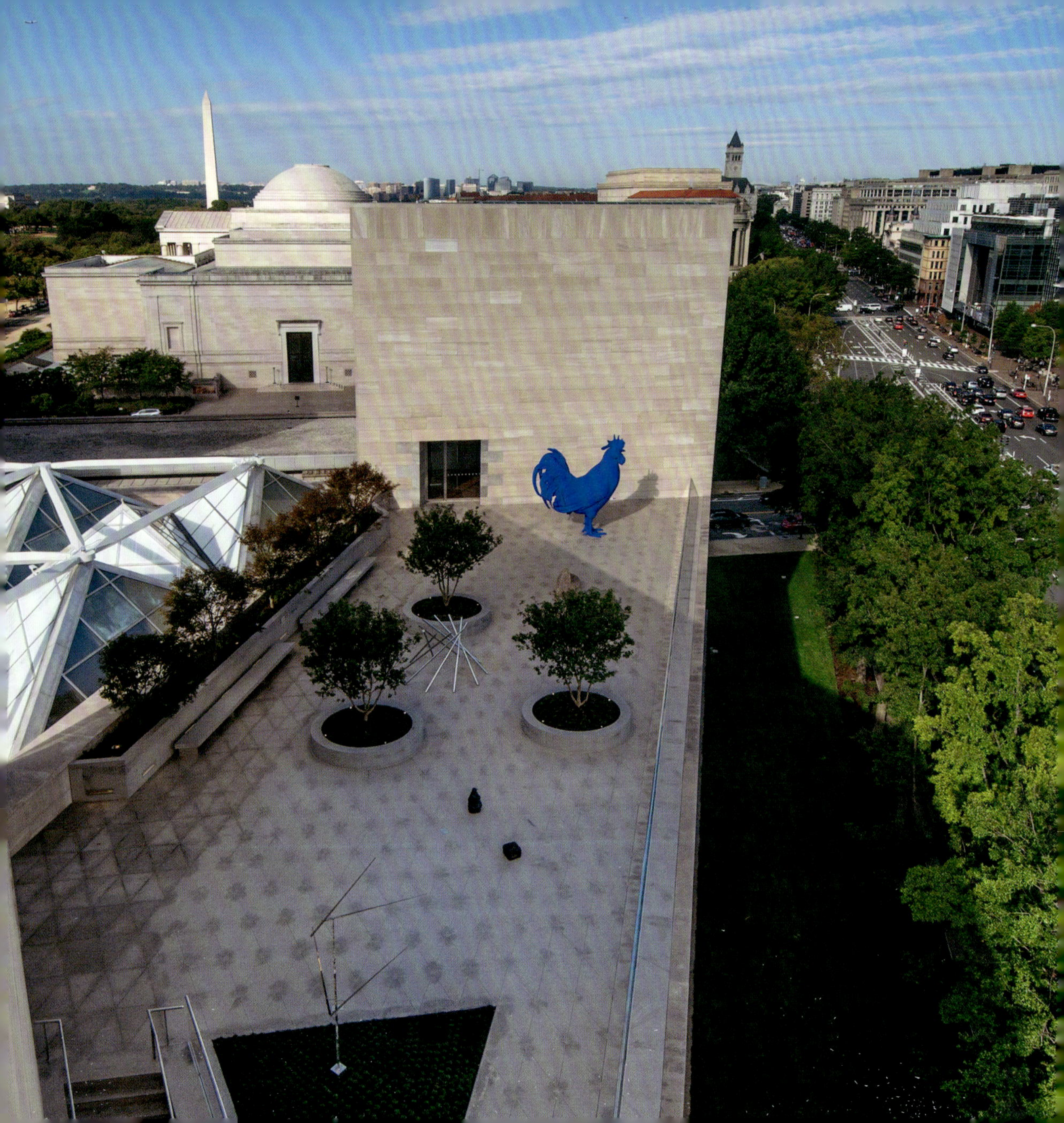

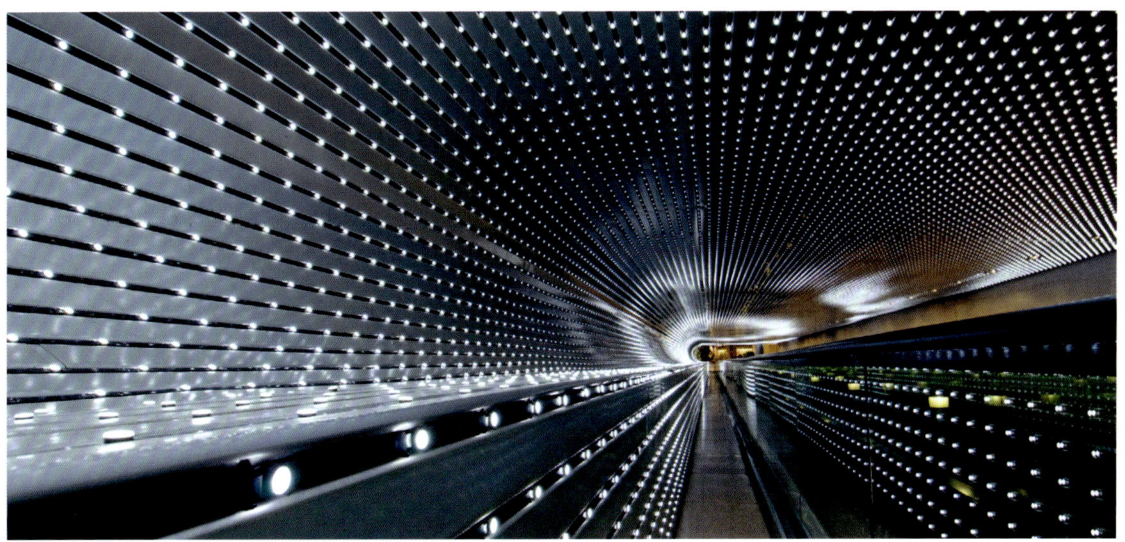

Did you know?
To enliven the underground walkway between the East and West Buildings, artist Leo Villareal installed strings of energy-efficient LED lights in the curved wall and ceiling slats. He programmed the thousands of lights in *Multiverse* to mimic wind, water, and other natural forces. The patterns are unlikely to ever repeat. At times, the lights race through the tunnel, seeming to take on a hyperspace effect.

The unusual trapezoidal shape of the site next to the original National Gallery of Art inspired the modern design of the East Building. Architect I. M. Pei divided the plot into an isosceles triangle with three towers (for exhibition and gallery spaces) and a right triangle (for a study center, library, and offices). He repeated the triangular motif throughout the building, from floor tiles to skylights. An innovative steel-and-glass structure of pyramid-shaped windows covers the 16,000 square feet of the Atrium, flooding the interior below with natural light. On the roof terrace, Katharina Fritsch's supersized blue rooster *Hahn/Cock* oversees contemporary sculptures and watches over Pennsylvania Avenue (left).

Slowly revolving at the center of the Atrium is a giant mobile that Alexander Calder created for the space. Pei worked with Calder and other artists to produce new works specifically for the East Building and its opening in 1978. Henry Moore's massive bronze sculpture stands outside the main entrance. Other site-specific works include Andy Goldsworthy's *Roof*, which is made of slate domes that blur the boundary between interior and exterior spaces. Leo Villareal's *Multiverse* is a sparkling tunnel of 41,000 programmed lights connecting the East and West Buildings (above).

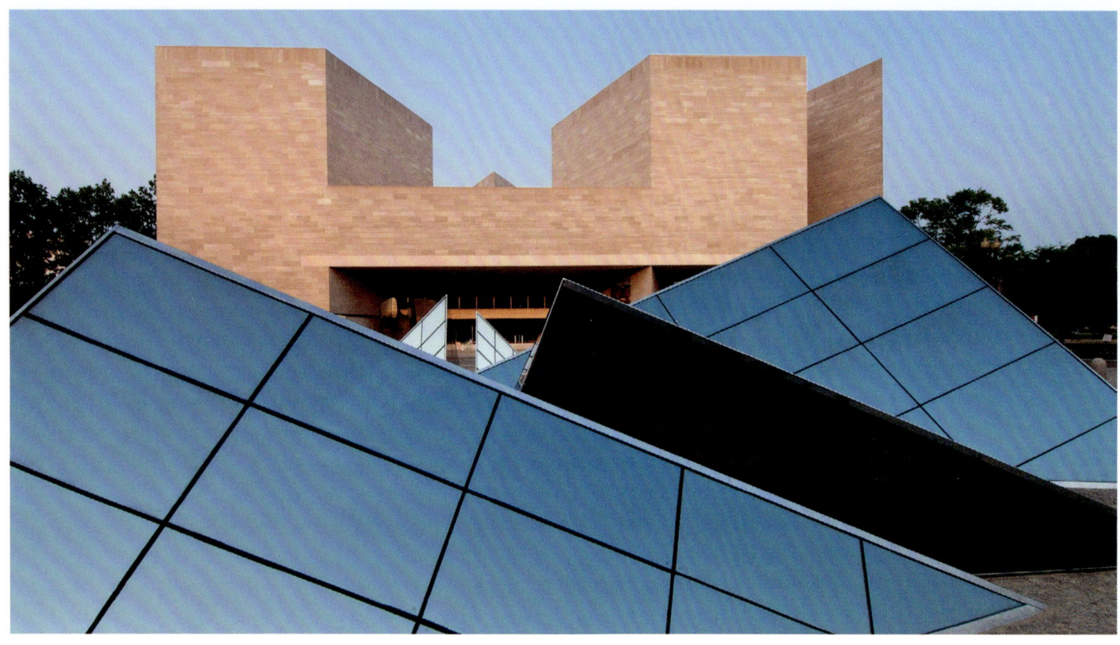

Surrounding the Atrium are five levels of modern and contemporary art. Works on view chart the evolution of painting and sculpture from the late 19th century to today. In these galleries you can trace the development of modernism, abstract expressionism, minimalism, pop, and so much more. Works by Carmen Herrera, Jaune Quick-to-See Smith, and Faith Ringgold join paintings by Mark Rothko, Jackson Pollock, and Andy Warhol.

The National Gallery's active exhibition program delves into all aspects of modern and contemporary art, offering in-depth explorations of individual artists and broader views of art created today.

Did you know?

Alexander Calder's huge mobile rotates serenely overhead (right)—but what makes it move? Air vents in the Atrium are directed at the artwork to ensure its continuous motion. Suspending the sculpture from the roof's glass-and-steel structure required a lightweight design. Engineered with thin sheet aluminum over a honeycomb frame, the mobile weighs about 920 pounds, roughly the same as a grand piano.

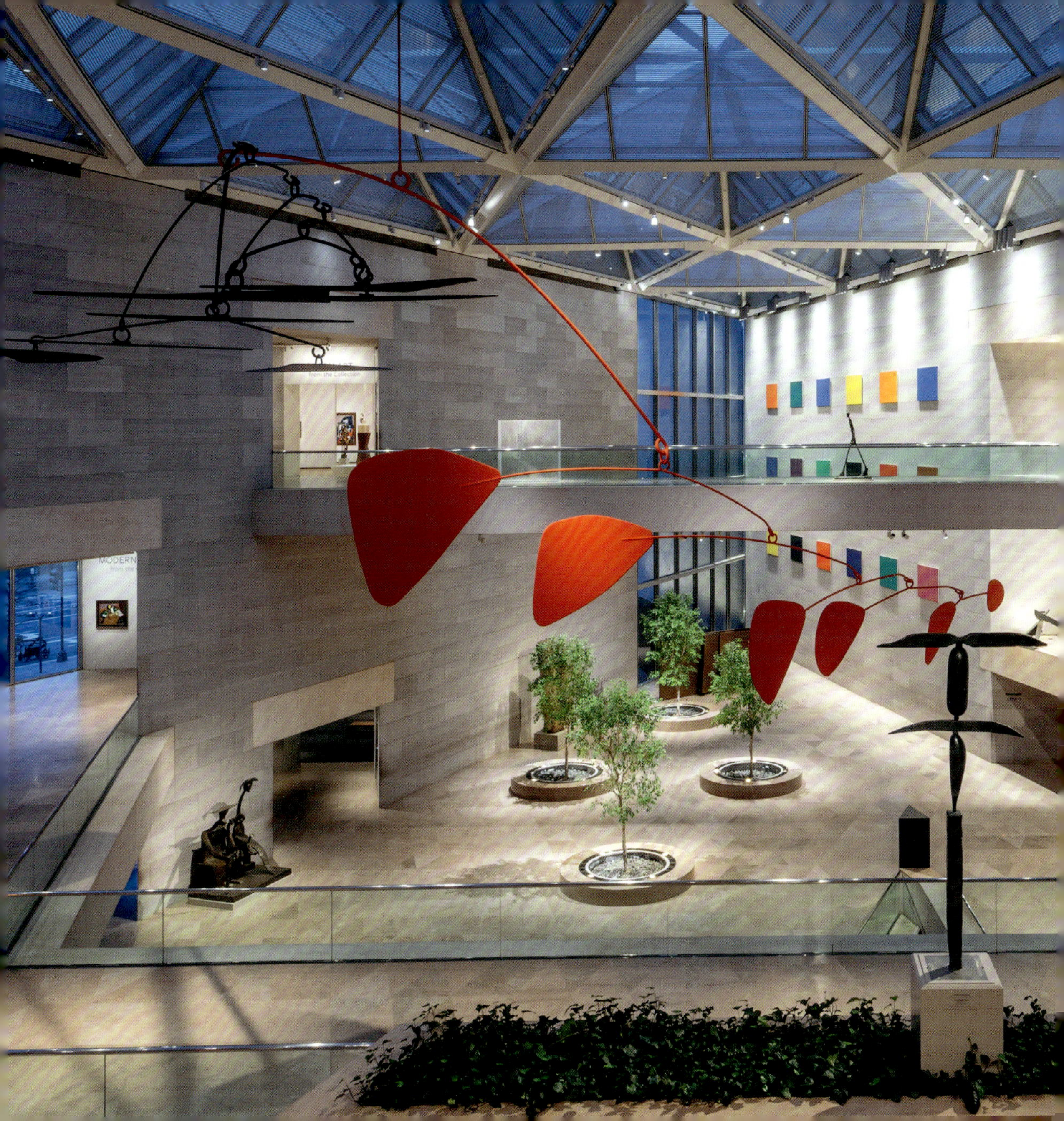
from the Collection
MODERN

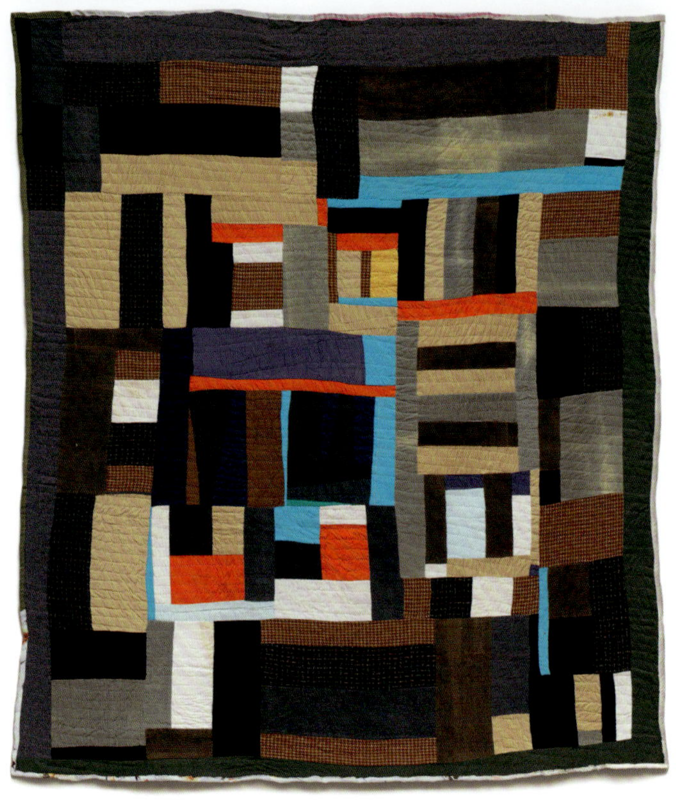

Mary Lee Bendolph
American, born 1935

Blocks and Strips
2002

wool, cotton, and corduroy

PATRONS' PERMANENT FUND AND GIFT OF THE SOULS GROWN DEEP FOUNDATION
2020.28.1

The rural African American community of Gee's Bend, Alabama, has been home to generations of quilters who pass on the traditions of their enslaved ancestors while they pursue innovation and self-expression. Among their leaders is Mary Lee Bendolph, an artist with scraps of cloth. She cuts worn and discarded clothing into geometric shapes—blocks and strips—to create vibrant abstract works. In this quilt, turquoise, red, and gold forms jump from a carefully arranged grid of denim and brown wool.

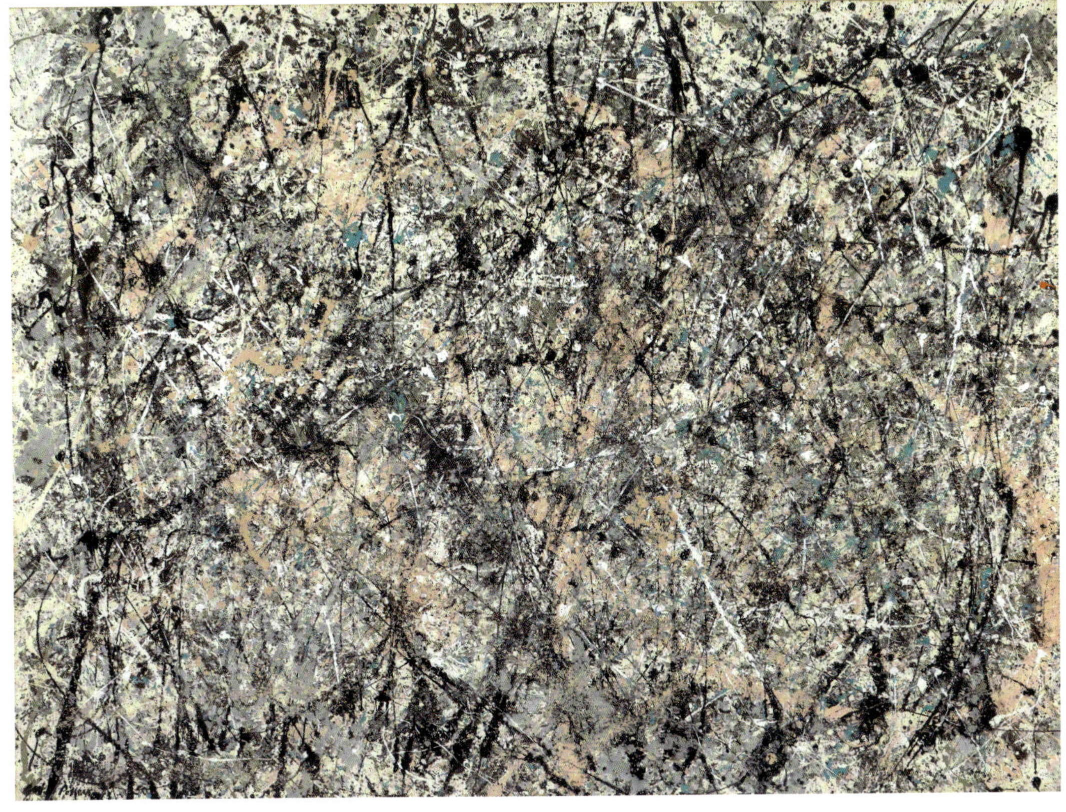

Jackson Pollock
American, 1912–1956

Number 1, 1950 (Lavender Mist)
1950

oil, enamel, and aluminum on canvas

AILSA MELLON BRUCE FUND
1976.37.1

Black, blue, white, silver, russet, and orange paint are here, but no lavender. The title, suggested by a critic who championed the artist, points our attention to light and color effects. Jackson Pollock's untraditional method of dripping, flinging, and pouring paint seemed random to a doubting public in the 1940s, but his technique was controlled. ("I deny the accident," he once said.) Moving over and around huge canvases spread on the floor, he aimed to be at one, physically and emotionally, with the process. Pollock's large, lyrical compositions are groundbreaking examples of abstract expressionist art in the mid-20th century.

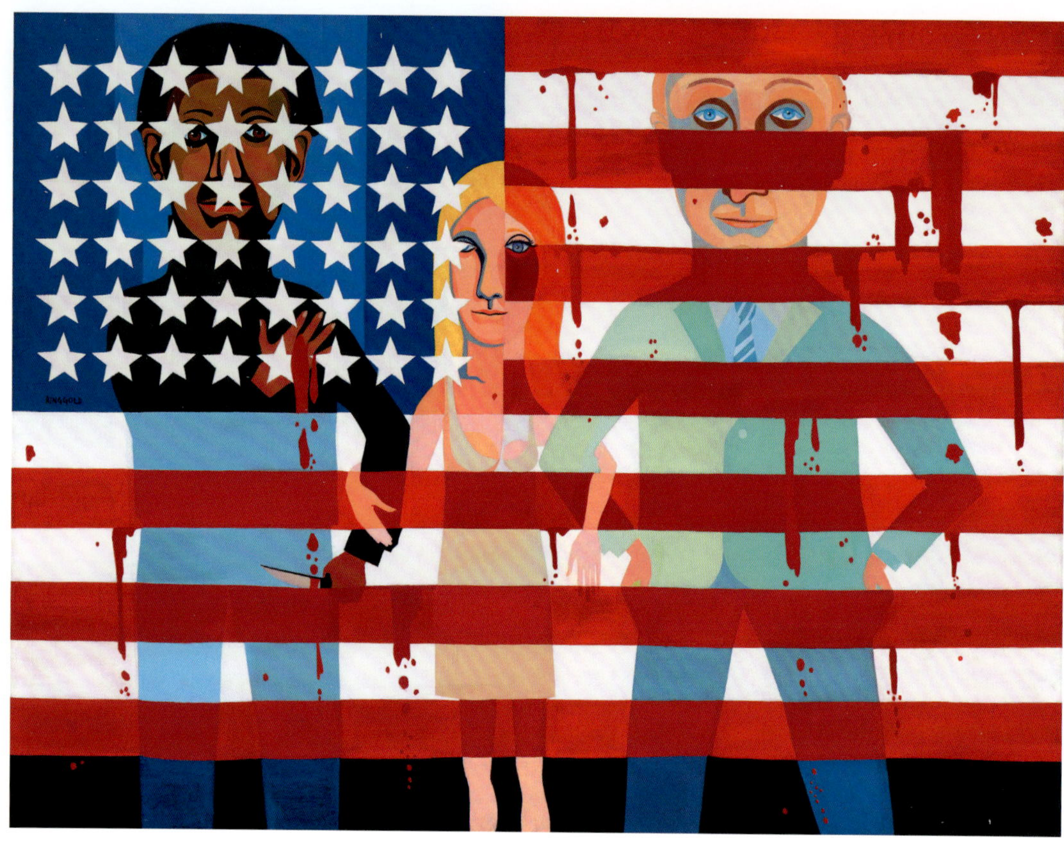

Faith Ringgold
American, 1930–2024

The American People Series #18: The Flag is Bleeding
1967

oil on canvas

GIFT OF GLENSTONE FOUNDATION AND PATRONS' PERMANENT FUND
2021.28.1

There is something subversive about seeing an American flag dripping with blood. Faith Ringgold knows that, and she doesn't shy away. The artist intentionally positions her three subjects behind the ghastly screen. The white people and Black man link arms, but this is not a scene of peace or reconciliation. The white man, with legs spread and hands on hips, poses like a gunslinger. The Black man holds a bloody knife. He looks like he's pledging allegiance to the flag, but blood seeps between his fingers at his heart. Made during the racial violence and political turbulence of the 1960s, this work seems to ask, Can we ever be united?

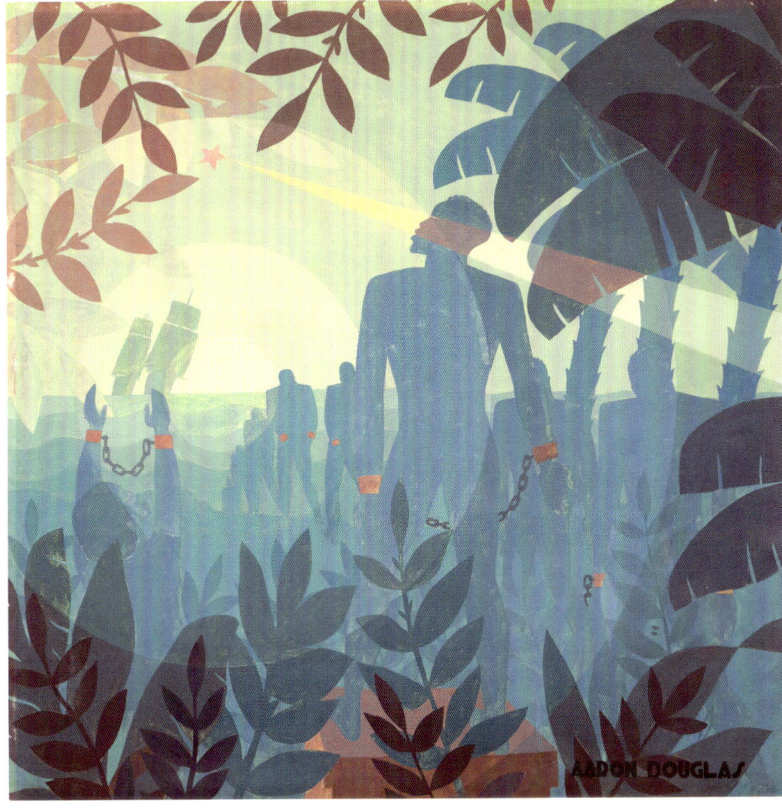

Aaron Douglas
American, 1899–1979

Into Bondage
1936

oil on canvas

CORCORAN COLLECTION (MUSEUM PURCHASE AND PARTIAL GIFT FROM THURLOW EVANS TIBBS, JR., THE EVANS-TIBBS COLLECTION, 1996)
2014.79.17

We glimpse the harrowing drama unfolding in this painting, as if we are crouching by the roots of the tropical foliage and peering through a space between the leaves. Our focus is on the anonymous silhouettes of men and women, their shackles more prominent than their features. They slouch toward waiting ships. We know the tragic outcome of their impending journey: enslavement in a distant country. A pulsating light on the horizon—a star—casts a bright beam on the large figure at center. Aaron Douglas, an artist of the Harlem Renaissance, acknowledges his ancestors' resilience and hope in the face of oppression.

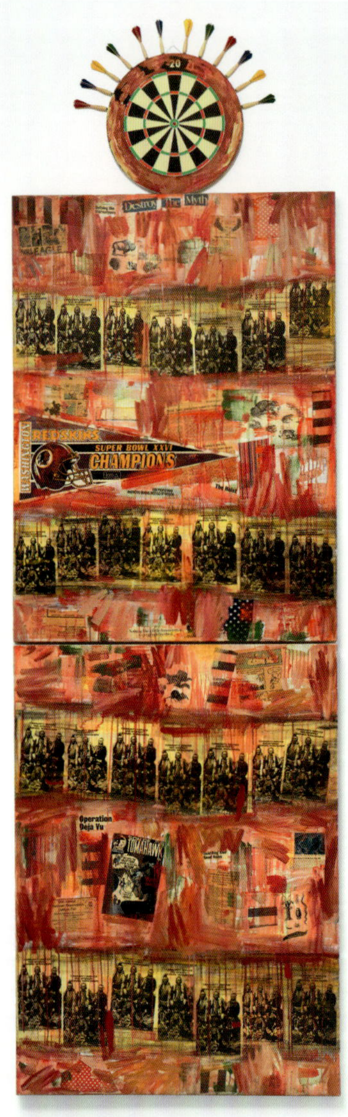

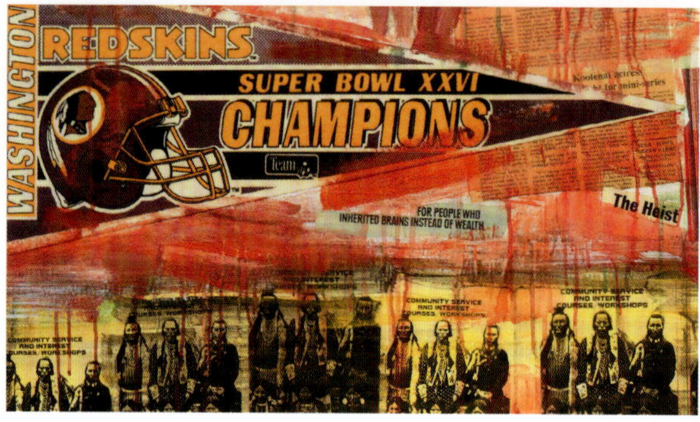

Jaune Quick-to-See Smith
Citizen of the Confederated Salish and Kootenai Nation, born 1940

Target
1992

mixed media on canvas

PURCHASED WITH FUNDS FROM EMILY AND MITCHELL RALES
2020.6.1

A target circled by darts resembles a headdress. Below it, repeated historical images of Indigenous people drip with bloodlike red paint. Native newspapers, a comic book, and a Super Bowl pennant featuring the former name of Washington's football team make it clear who is the target: Native Americans. Jaune Quick-to-See Smith's anger is clearly felt in the violent brushes of color. *Target* confronts complex issues of identity and exploitation.

Henri Matisse
French, 1869–1954

Open Window, Collioure
1905

oil on canvas

COLLECTION OF MR. AND MRS. JOHN HAY WHITNEY
1998.74.7

A painting may provide a "window" into a different world. Here, the painting is itself a window, and it reveals a world dizzy with color and movement. Over the flowerpots on the sill and through the leaves of the ivy, we see sailboats bobbing off the Mediterranean coastal town of Collioure in France. The windowpanes, opened inward, reflect large blocks of salmon, green, and lavender from the interior walls. Thick staccato marks suggest foliage, water, and boats. This work was thought to be shocking in the early 20th century, and its creator, Henri Matisse, was dubbed a *fauve,* or wild beast.

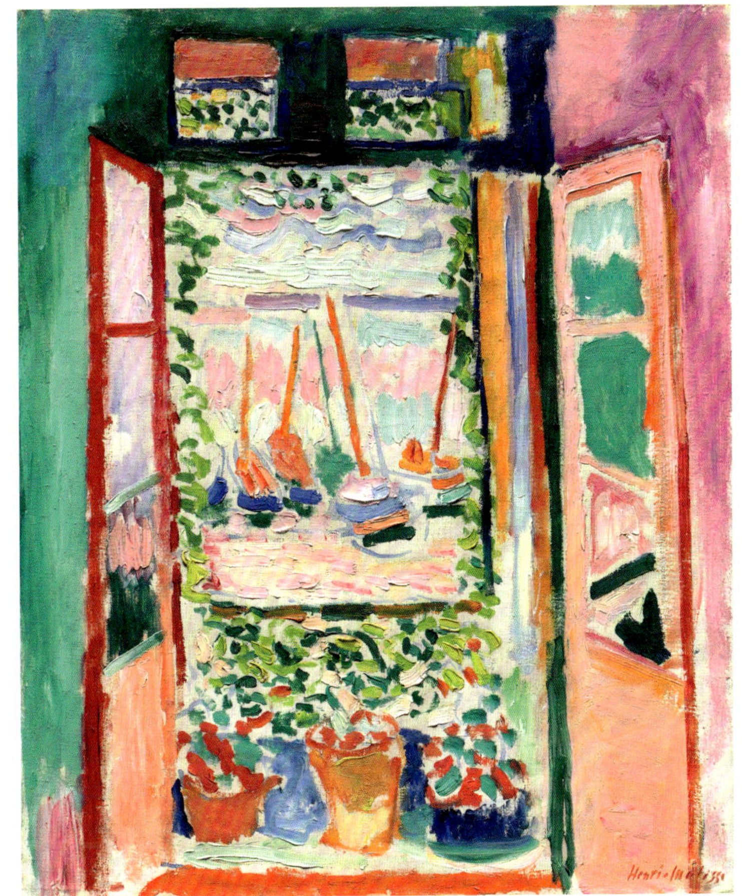

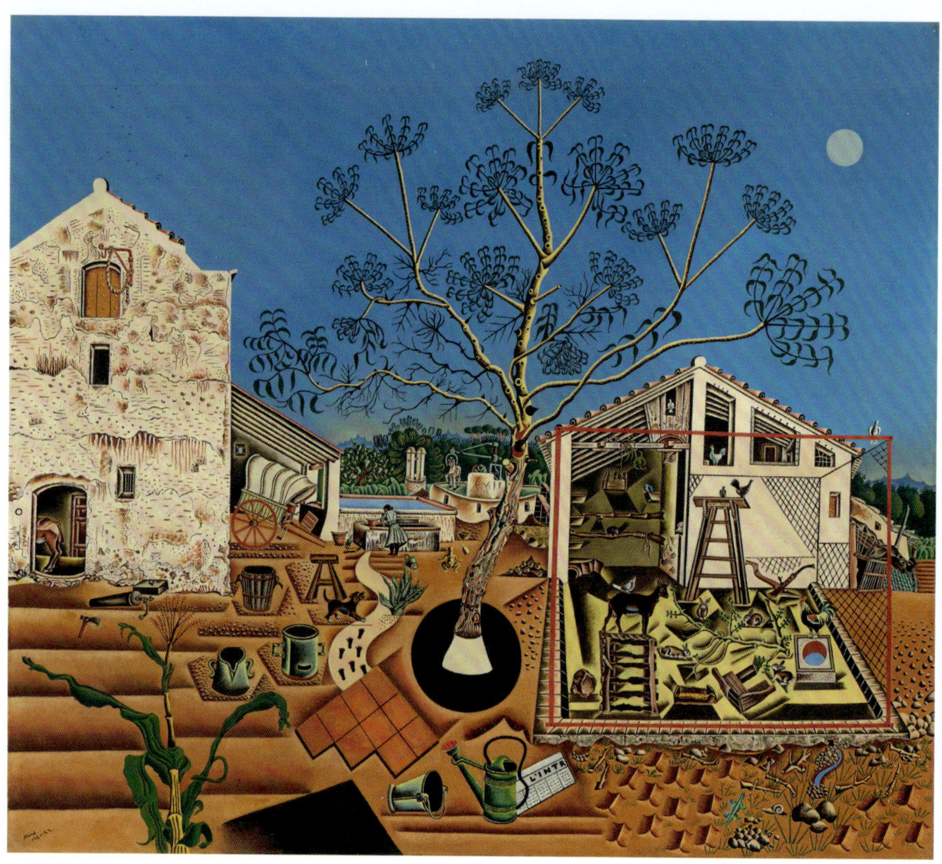

Joan Miró
Spanish, 1893–1983

The Farm
1921–1922

oil on canvas

GIFT OF MARY HEMINGWAY
1987.18.1

This could be a scene from a children's book, but the story is a strange one. At first glance, everything looks ordinary. Crops spring from the ground, animals are in the shed, and a donkey turns a millstone to grind grain—but what about the newspaper under the watering can or the footprints that suddenly stop on the path? These puzzling pictograms of daily life on Joan Miró's family farm in Montroig, Spain, invite us into a magical world. The dreamlike images attracted author Ernest Hemingway, the painting's first owner, and did much to inspire the surrealist movement a few years later.

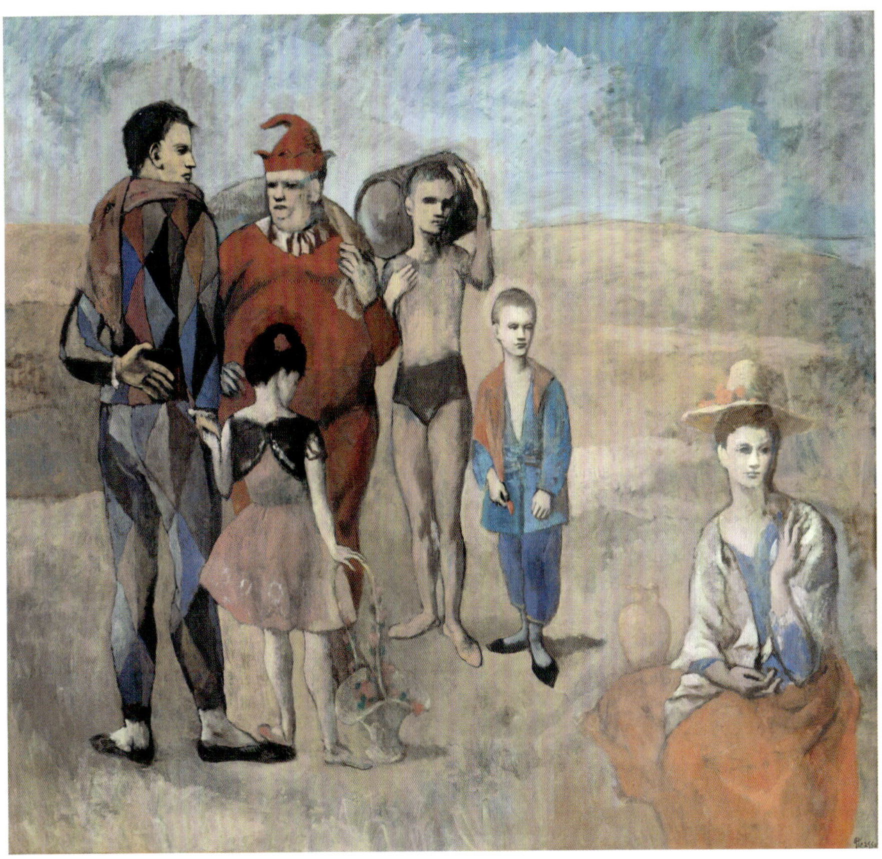

Pablo Picasso
Spanish, 1881–1973

Family of Saltimbanques
1905

oil on canvas

CHESTER DALE COLLECTION
1963.10.190

This is no "family" in the usual sense. A harlequin, a jester, a young man in a leotard, a boy in a blue costume, a girl in a tutu with a basket, and a woman in a flowered hat are arranged in this rose-hued landscape. They may be related, but they make no eye contact. These *saltimbanques,* or circus performers, seem to be haunted by their own thoughts. When Pablo Picasso painted this large canvas, the young Spanish artist had recently arrived in Paris. Like this band of entertainers, he and his creative friends were living on the margins of society. Picasso added his own distinctive profile to the harlequin.

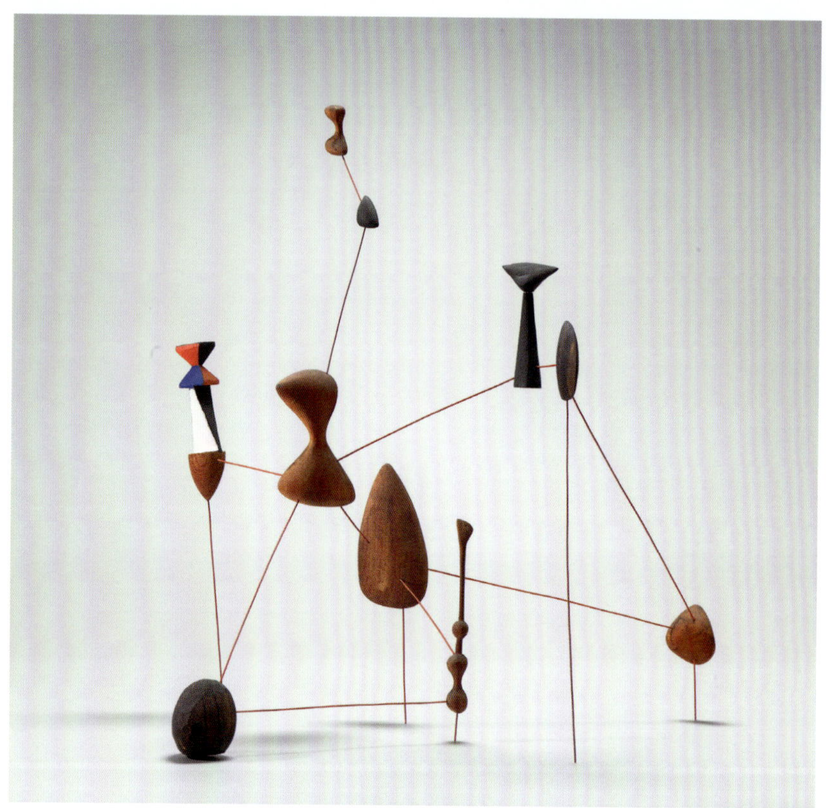

Alexander Calder
American, 1898–1976

Vertical Constellation with Bomb

1943

wire, wood, and paint

GIFT OF MR. AND MRS. KLAUS G. PERLS
1996.120.8

Alexander Calder's interest in open composition led him to create a series of delicate objects made of carved wood and wire. Artist Marcel Duchamp and writer James Johnson Sweeney proposed the name "constellations" for them. This is the most complex one. His uncharacteristic use of wood was due to the scarcity of scrap metal during World War II. Unlike his suspended mobiles, which drift slowly through space, many of Calder's constellations do not move, yet their organic shapes cast shadows that shift with the light. The appearance of these open, linear structures constantly alters as we move past them.

Mark Rothko
American, born Russia (now Latvia), 1903–1970

Untitled
1949

pigmented hide glue and oil on canvas

GIFT OF THE MARK ROTHKO FOUNDATION, INC.
1986.43.138

Mark Rothko did not want to explain what his works mean, and he often chose to leave them untitled. He preferred to use color and composition not for their own sake but to convey profound states of human existence. At the time he painted this canvas, Rothko had just settled on what would become his classic style: a large format featuring soft-edged rectangular forms set on a field or background of a single color. Here, the contrasting hues of green, dark orange, black, yellow, and plum placed against a light yellow background were intended to spark emotion and to suggest, as Rothko noted, universal themes of "tragedy, ecstasy, doom."

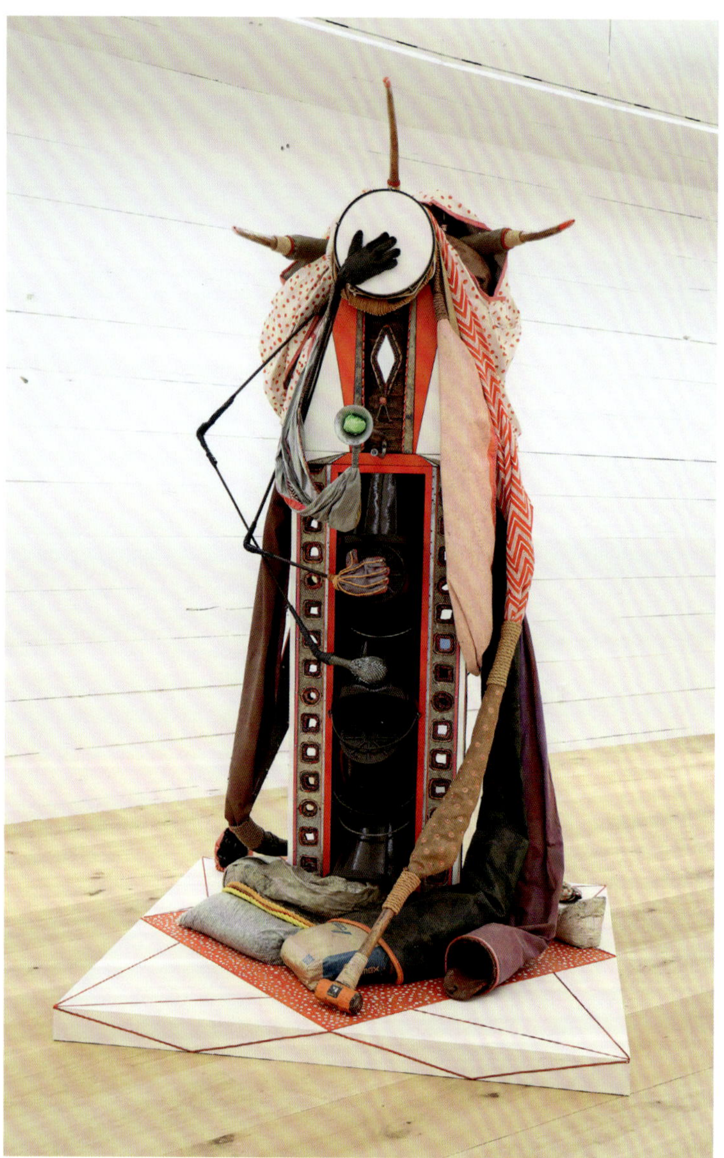

Daniel Lind-Ramos
Puerto Rican, born 1953

Figura de Poder (Power Figure)
2016–2020

mirrors, concrete blocks, cement bag, sledgehammer, construction stones bag, paint bucket, wood panels, palm tree trunk, burlap, leather, ropes, sequin, awning, plastic ropes, fabric, trumpet, pins, duct tape, maracas, sneaker, tambourine, working gloves, boxing gloves, and acrylic

NEW CENTURY FUND
2022.6.1

The rhythms and traditions of everyday life in Loíza, the Afro-Puerto Rican community where Daniel Lind-Ramos was raised, inspire his intricate assemblages. This towering figure made of found objects—a tambourine, buckets, maracas, horns, rope, boxing gloves, a sneaker, and more—is dressed in festive clothing reminiscent of the costumes worn by revelers during Loíza's Fiesta de Santiago Apóstol. As we explore the details of this work, we realize power takes many forms: play, labor, music, protest, and spiritual devotion.

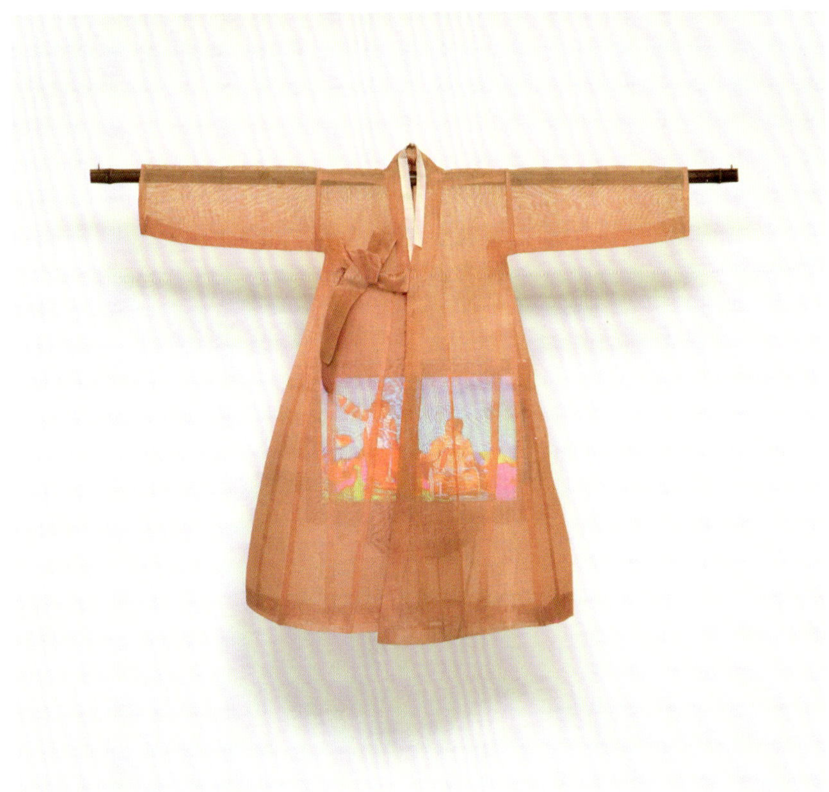

Nam June Paik
American, born South Korea, 1932–2006

Ommah
2005

one-channel video installation on 19-inch LCD monitor, silk robe

GIFT OF THE COLLECTORS COMMITTEE
2010.62.1

A silk robe hangs with arms outstretched. It is the kind of garment worn by privileged Korean boys a century ago, but there's a twist. The delicate fabric acts as a gauzy curtain for an LCD TV monitor. A video of Korean American girls in traditional costume is interrupted by TV shows, games, and concert tapes twisted and distorted by a video synthesizer that Nam June Paik helped to invent. Created a year before Paik's death, this intriguing work alludes to his heritage—*ommah* means "mother" in Korean—and his long career as a multimedia artist and acknowledged founder of the medium of video sculpture.

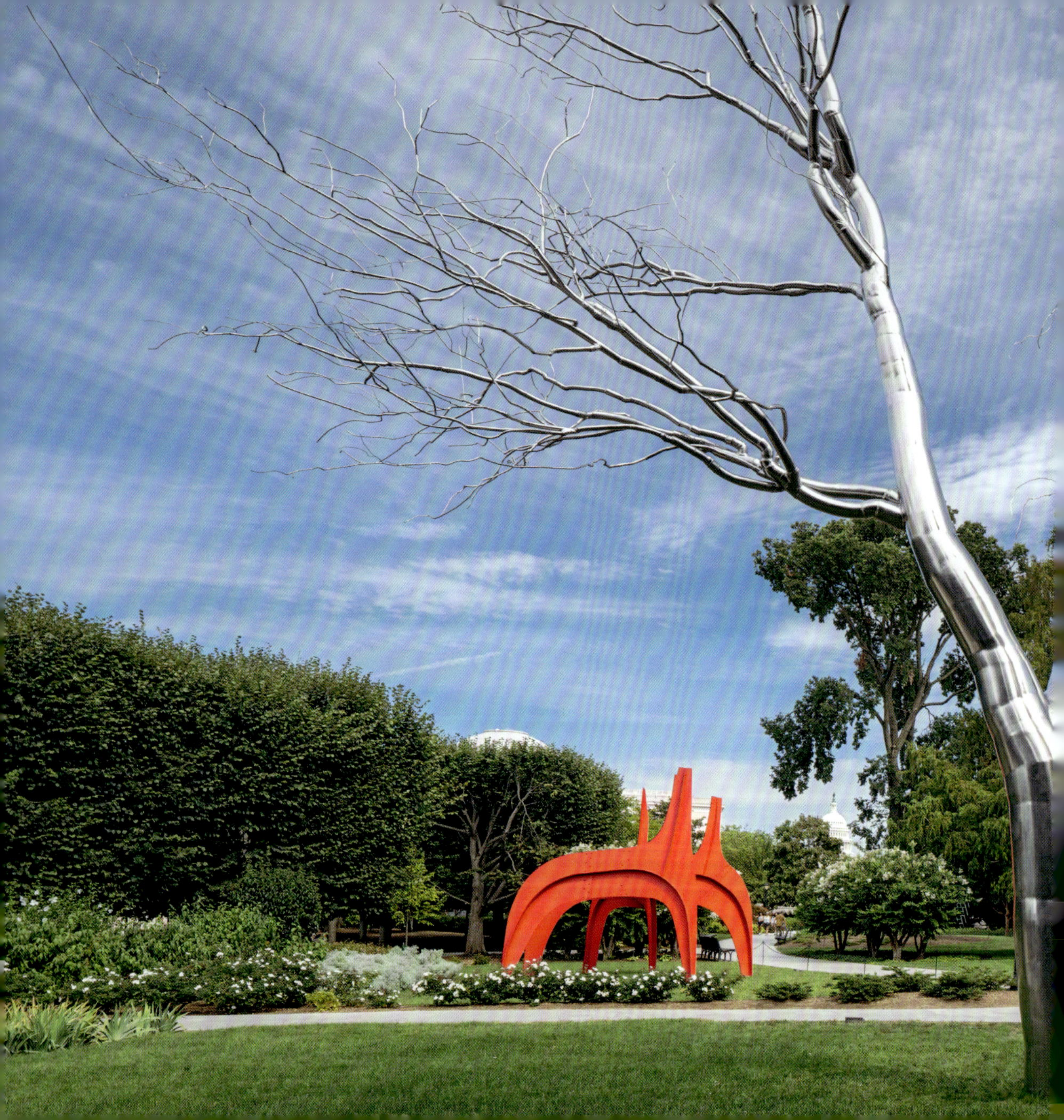

Sculpture Garden

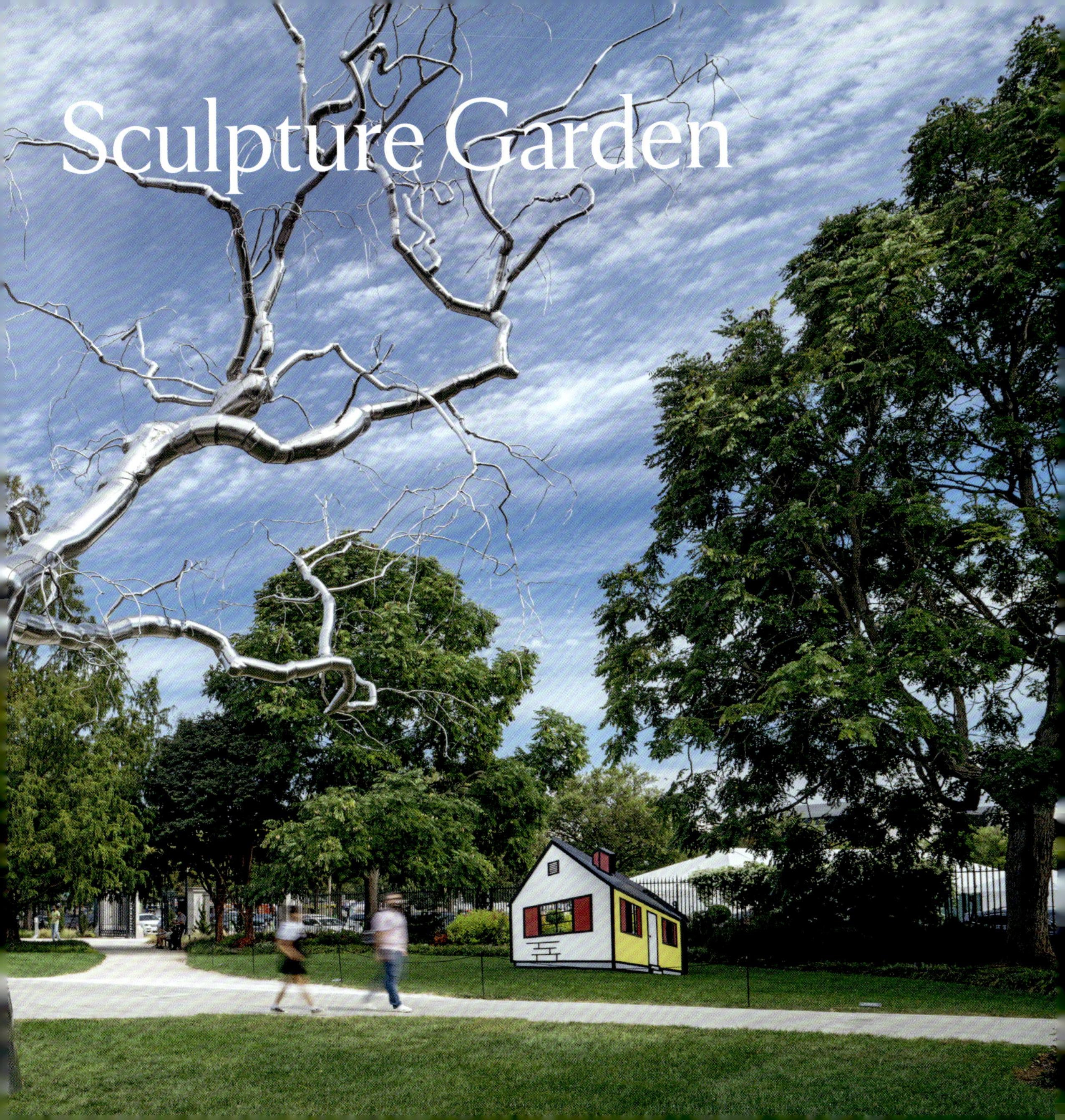

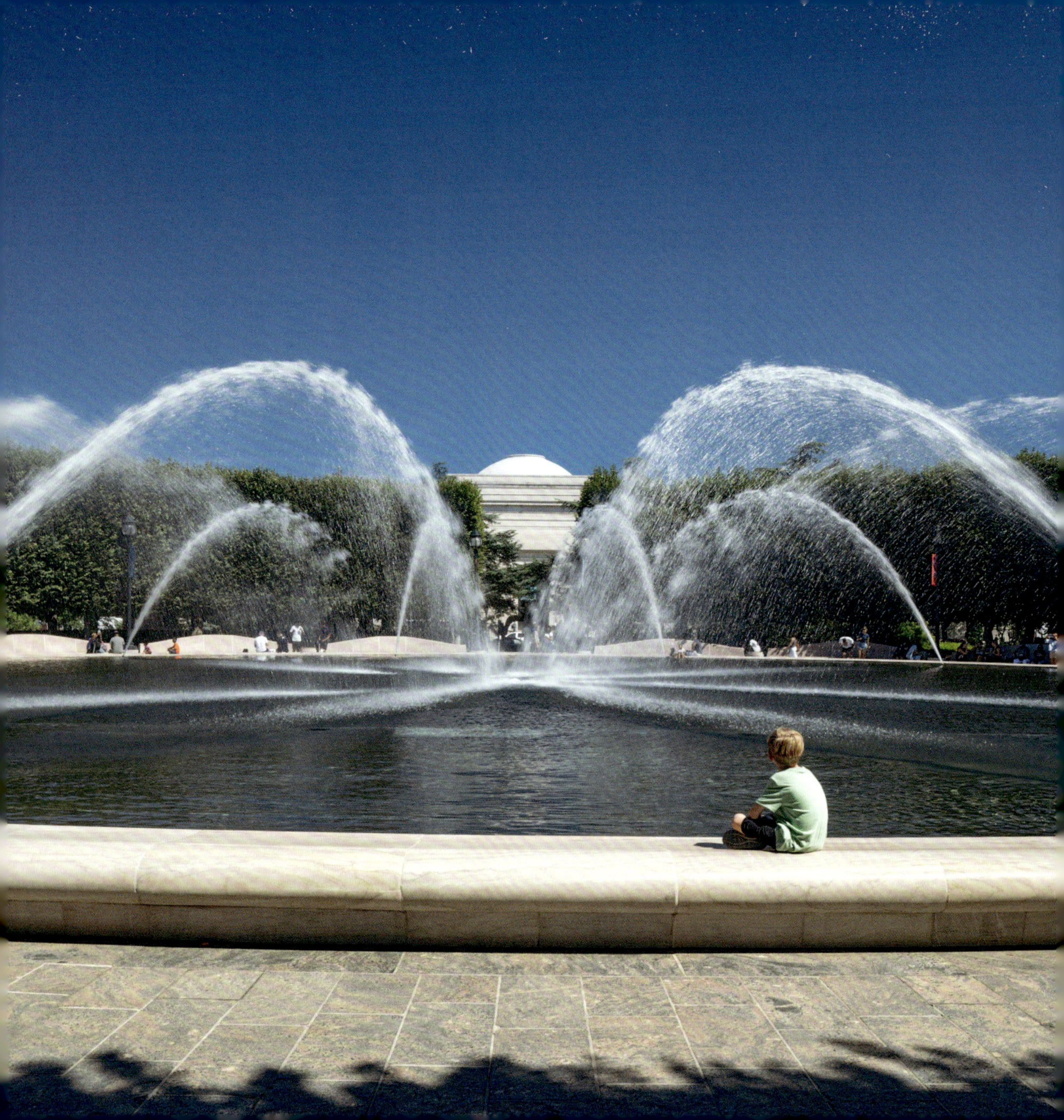

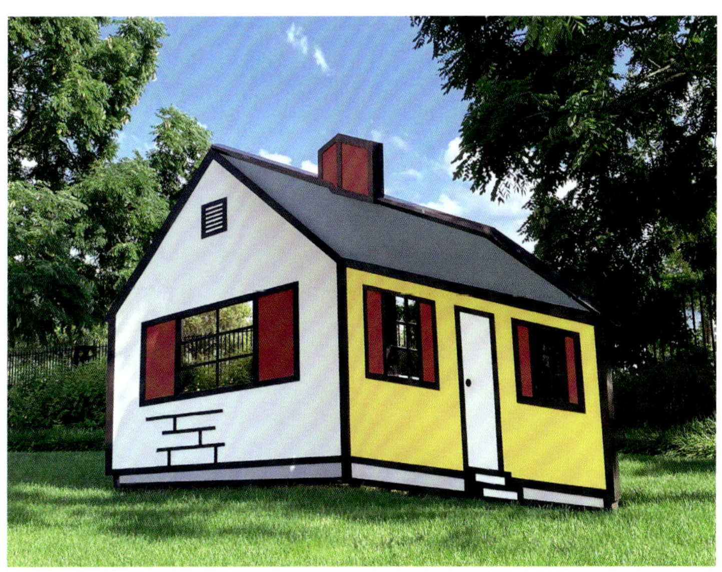

Did you know?
Set within a circle of linden trees, the Sculpture Garden's fountain serves double duty on the National Mall. During Washington's humid summers, the fountain and its eight arcs of spraying water provide a place to relax and renew. It's also the backdrop for the National Gallery's popular outdoor concerts. In the winter, the fountain is transformed into a public ice rink for skaters of all ages.

To the west of the National Gallery's buildings is the open-air Sculpture Garden designed by landscape architect Laurie D. Olin. This six-acre outdoor gallery centers around a circular reflecting fountain. The fountain and its round shape echo the rotunda in the West Building. This engaging water feature also brings to mind the waterfall on the plaza between the East and West Buildings. The pink Tennessee marble used in the entrance gateways, benches, and fountain basin further connects the Sculpture Garden with the rest of the National Gallery campus.

Walking along the pathways of the Sculpture Garden, you'll encounter more than 20 large-scale works by modern sculptors. With *Thinker on a Rock*, Barry Flanagan playfully substitutes a giant hare, lost in thought, for the male figure in Auguste Rodin's iconic sculpture *The Thinker*. Other artworks might make you pause and look—and look again. Claes Oldenburg and Coosje van Bruggen's towering *Typewriter Eraser, Scale X* provokes laughter and perhaps memories of life before computers. With *House I*, Roy Lichtenstein creates an optical illusion: the flat, painted aluminum "house" seems to change shape as you walk by it (above).

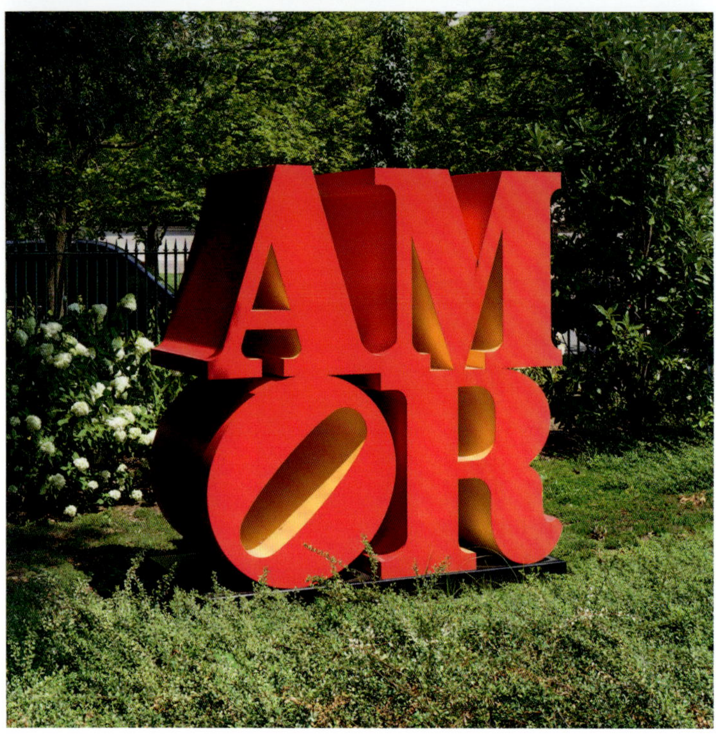

The outdoor setting offers surprises throughout the year. Set among the ever-changing colors of flowering plants and trees are more sculptures by Marc Chagall, Joan Miró, Tony Smith, Ellsworth Kelly, Sol LeWitt, Alfredo Halegua (right), and other renowned artists. Robert Indiana's red and yellow *AMOR*, based on his widely recognized *LOVE* sculpture, has become a favorite spot for taking photos (above).

The Sculpture Garden brings together art, architecture, nature, and relaxation in the heart of the nation's capital.

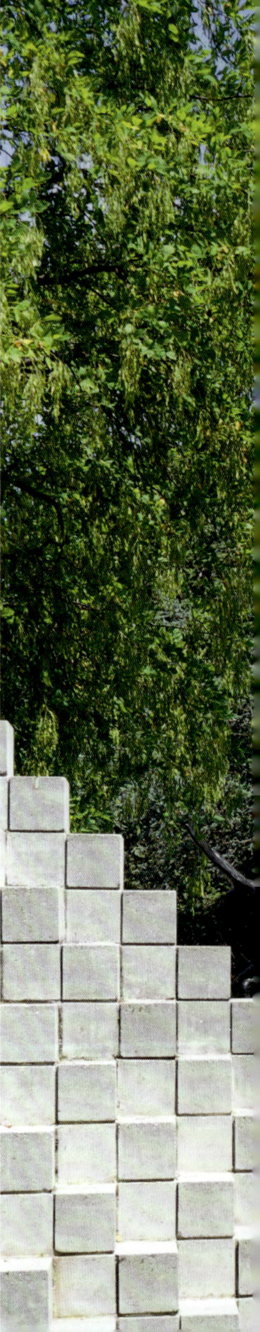

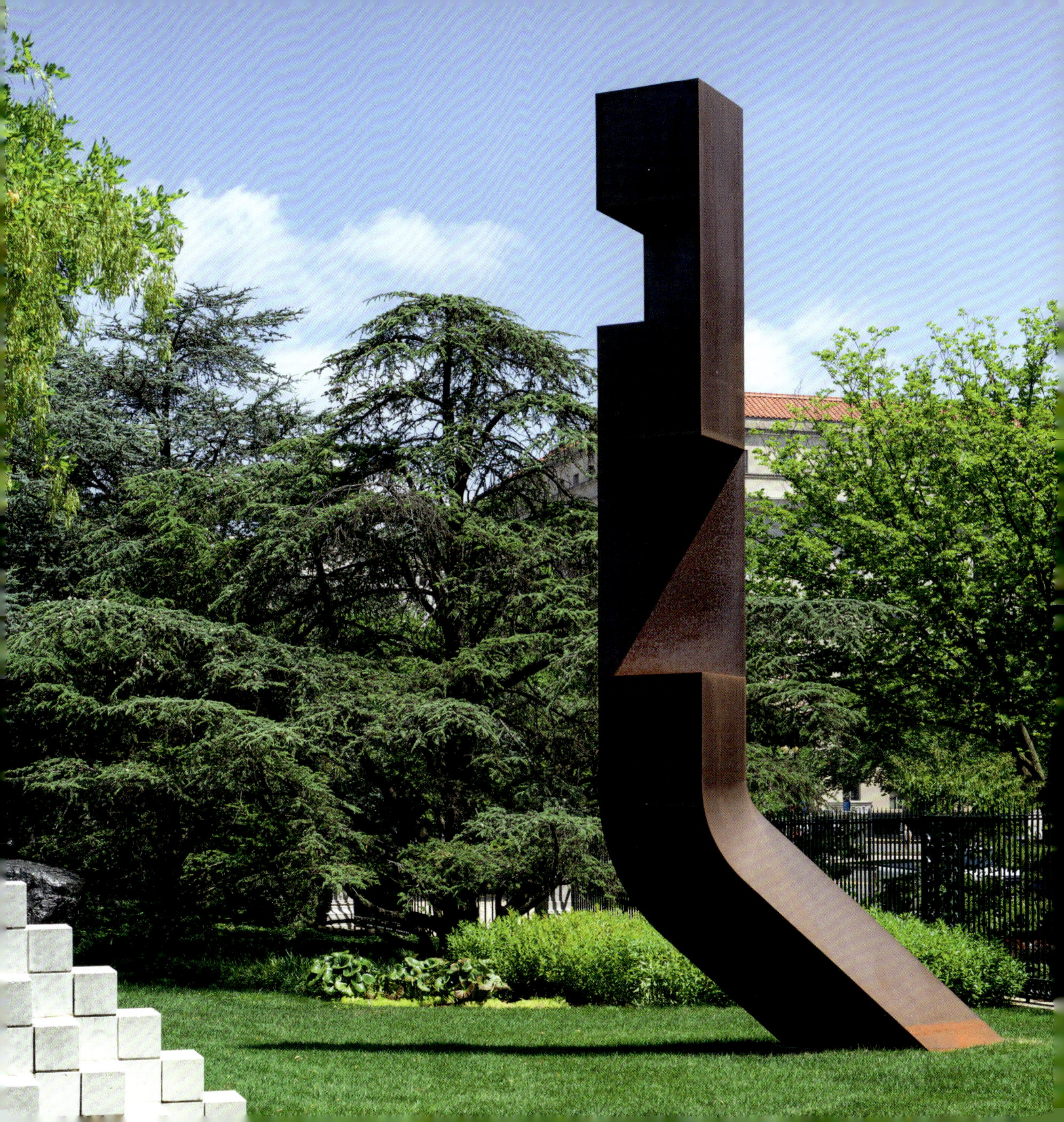

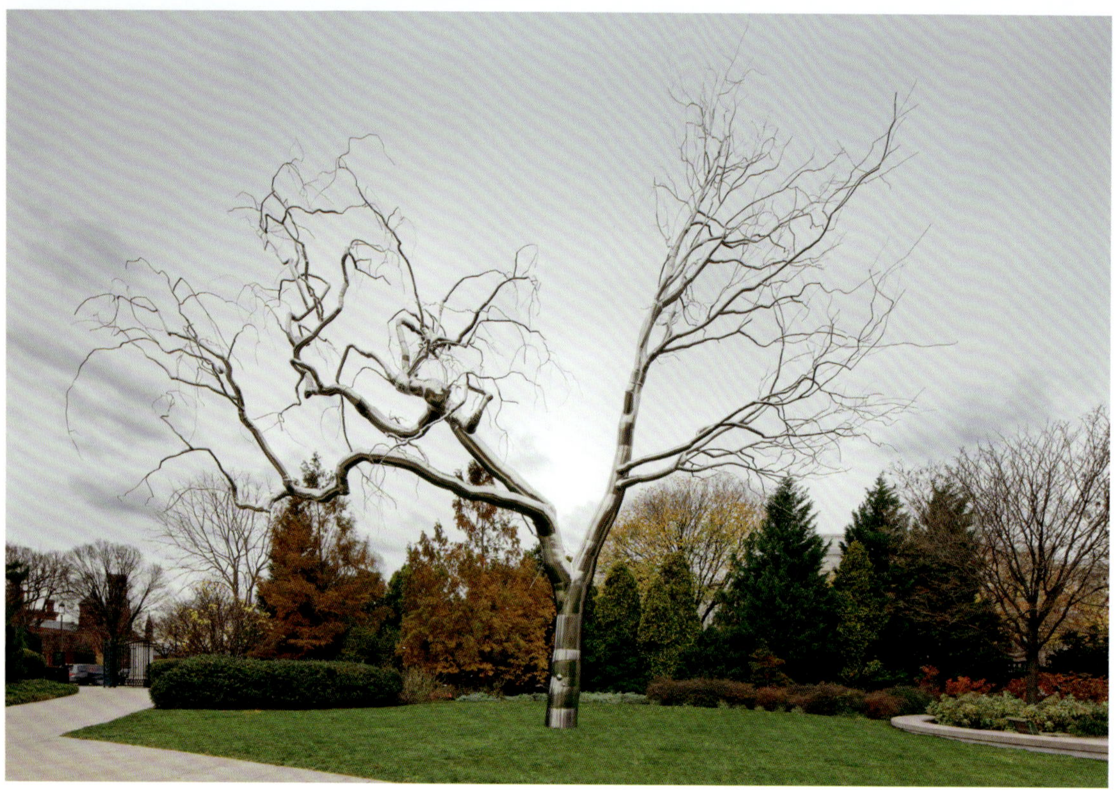

Roxy Paine
American, born 1966

Graft
2008–2009

stainless steel and concrete

GIFT OF VICTORIA AND ROBERT SANT
2009.109.1

There is a leafless tree in the Sculpture Garden. Made of polished stainless steel by artist Roxy Paine, this tree literally outshines the natural beauty surrounding it. Yet, it is hardly natural in form or materials. Branches on one side soar skyward, while limbs on the opposite side are twisted. *Graft*, the title of this work, refers to the horticultural practice of joining the bud, stem, or root of one tree to another to repair or propagate it. The title might also be a pun referring to a form of political corruption.

Claes Oldenburg
American, born Sweden,
1929–2022

Coosje van Bruggen
American, born Holland,
1942–2009

Typewriter Eraser, Scale X
model 1998, fabricated 1999

painted stainless steel and fiberglass

GIFT OF THE MORRIS AND
GWENDOLYN CAFRITZ FOUNDATION
1998.150.1

We might be puzzled about the purpose of this monumental sculpture until we read its title. Before the invention of the delete key on the computer keyboard, the humble typewriter eraser allowed people to rub out mistakes on typing paper. The end with the pink wheel erased the error; the blue brush swept away the eraser "crumbs." Claes Oldenburg was intrigued by this item from his childhood. He and Coosje van Bruggen recreated the eraser at enormous scale, giving it a windswept motion to ensure it would not be forgotten.

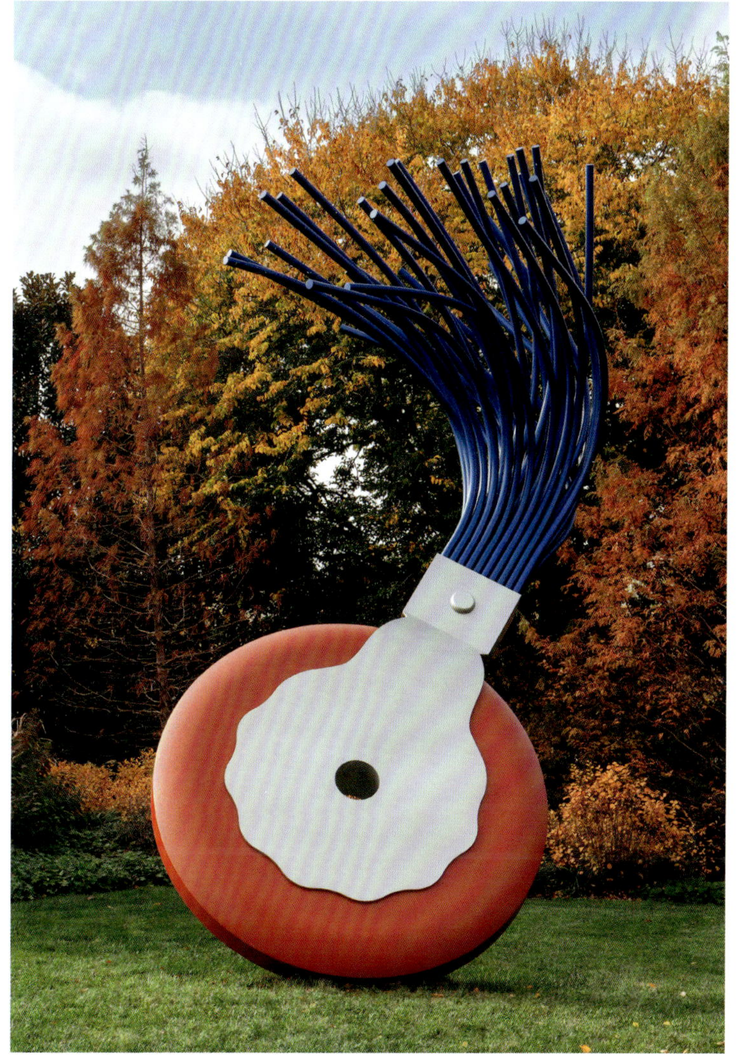

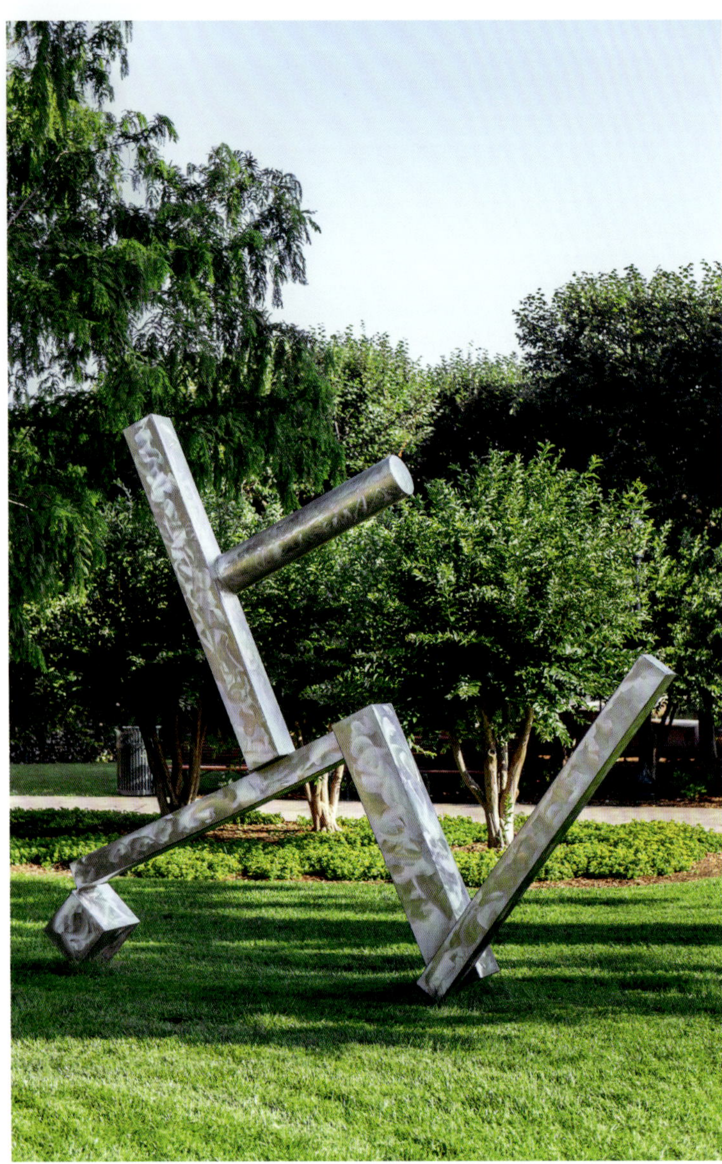

David Smith
American, 1906–1965

Cubi XXVI
1965

stainless steel

AILSA MELLON BRUCE FUND
1978.14.1

Before he became an artist, David Smith was a welder in a car factory. Can you tell? We know this steel sculpture is welded together, but the geometric forms seem precariously balanced. A little square cube bears much of the weight. Above it, a tall vertical piece leans back a bit too far while a cylinder reaches for stability. The burnished surface of the sculpture reflects light, so the work appears to change from different angles. *Cubi XXVI* also picks up the colors of the Sculpture Garden and the sky above it.

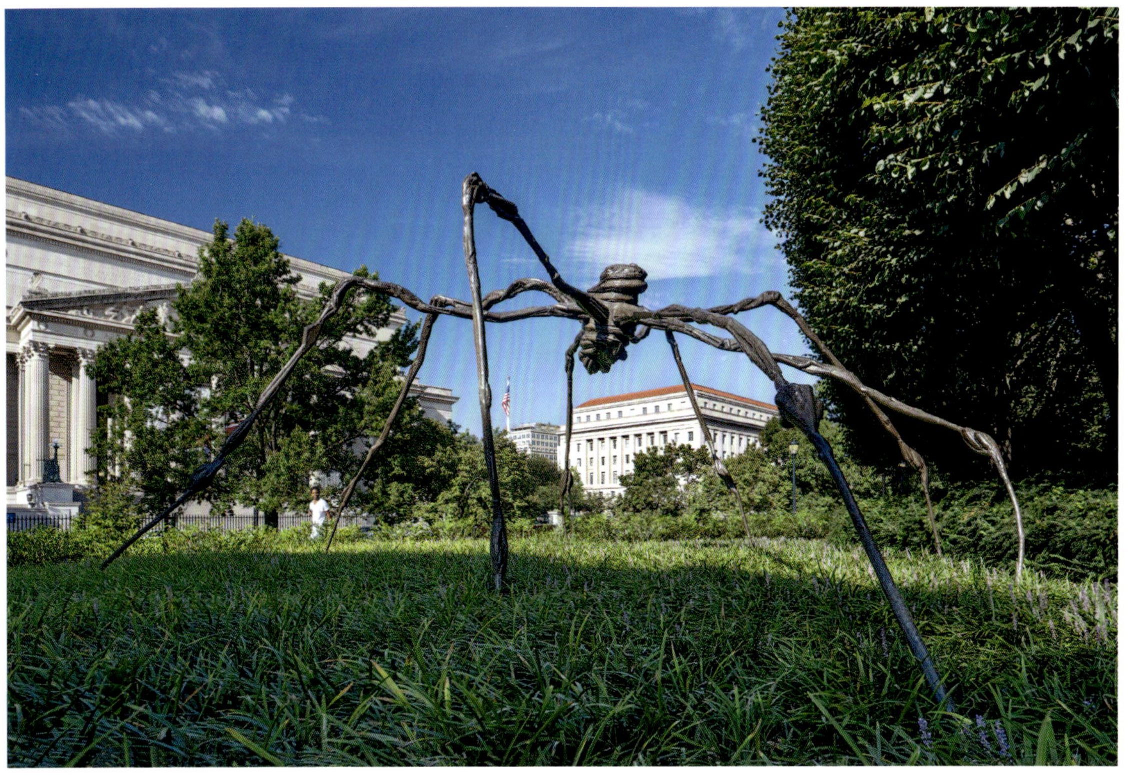

Louise Bourgeois
American, born France,
1911–2010

Spider
1996, cast 1997

bronze with silver nitrate patina

GIFT OF THE MORRIS AND
GWENDOLYN CAFRITZ FOUNDATION
1997.136.1

Looming behind one of the paths is a towering spider made of bronze. The eight legs, extending in every direction, are firmly planted in the ground and hold the tiny body aloft. This massive arachnid might seem frightening, but the elegant creature also inspires awe. Louise Bourgeois started making spider sculptures in the 1990s. She chose this animal as a subject because it reminded her of her mother, who "was deliberate, clever, patient, soothing, reasonable, dainty, subtle, indispensable, neat, and as useful as a spider."